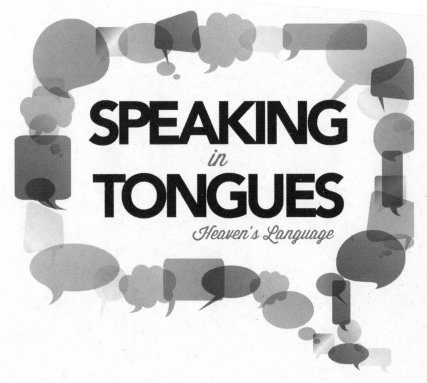

SPEAKING
in
TONGUES
Heaven's Language

ROBERT ENGELHARDT

Bridge-Logos
Alachua, Florida 32615

Bridge-Logos
Alachua, FL 32615 USA

Speaking In Tongues
Heaven's Language
by Robert Engelhardt

Printed in the USA

Library of Congress Control Number: 2013951760
ISBN: 978-1-61036-119-4

AN EQUIPPING PUBLICATION OF
PASTOR BOB ENGELHARDT MINISTRIES

To Contact the Author

CATSKILL MOUNTAIN CHRISTIAN CENTER
PO BOX 26 | 629 Main Street | Margaretville, NY 12455
845.586.4848 | cmcconline@yahoo.com
www.cmcconline.org

Dedicated to Nancy

Praise for *Speaking in Tongues*

Charismatic churches have too often replaced the power of the Holy Spirit's gifts with technology and the arts— mistaking talent for anointing. The gift of tongues enables us to communicate with the realm of Heaven and bring that powerfully to play in the Earth. Tongues allow you to pray effectively when stress, pressure, or frustration makes your words inadequate. I have also found when I am overwhelmed by the power and presence of God, that praying or singing in tongues allows me to worship beyond what my words can possibly express.

Praying in tongues requires faith. Praying in tongues daily as a devotional practice requires great faith. Bob Engelhardt is a man who has put theory into practice and seen abundant fruitfulness in his own life. *Speaking in Tongues* is more than an academic study on the relevance of tongues; it is a heartfelt, forthright, honest testimony from a man of integrity seeking to challenge the Church to invest in praying in tongues devotionally. I know this man. I agree with his message. I invite you to read *Speaking in Tongues* with an open mind and access all God has available to you as a believer.

Dr. John P. Kelly
President & CEO of LEAD
Convening Apostle, ICA

Praise for *Speaking in Tongues*

Speaking in Tongues offers every believer a practical, spiritual understanding of the purpose, use, and joy of speaking in tongues. Pastor Bob Engelhardt has given charismatics and Pentecostals alike a wonderful guide for deepening a Christian's relationship with the Holy Spirit through a vital prayer life of praying in the Spirit. I encourage every pastor and lay person desiring a more powerful and impactful prayer life to be equipped by everything imparted in this book!

Dr. Larry Keefauver
Bestselling Author | International Teacher

Bob Engelhardt is a practical man of faith. He believes the Word of God is literal and relevant for today. He makes a powerful case for the devotional practice of praying in tongues from the perspective of Scripture as well from personal testimony. *Speaking in Tongues* demonstrates—from Genesis all the way to Revelation—the creative presence of the Holy Spirit at work to separate light from darkness. A thought-provoking and powerful resource for believers, this book shows you how praying in tongues allows you to pray in agreement with Heaven free from the filter of your own experience and perspective.

Wendy K. Walters
Speaker | Author | Consultant

Contents

PREFACE

Have We Lost a Precious Gift?

In the work of Christianity it is easy to forget that ours is a spiritual business. So much emphasis is placed on form and function, we tend to look through our western lens for the immediate, measurable payoff of any spiritual investment. If we don't see fast profit in terms of our own needs and desires, we quickly sell the asset and look for something more lucrative. We expect spiritual payoffs to be something akin to Wall Street day-traders or even lottery winnings!

I remember the story of a young guy who, for a time, trained hard spiritually. He memorized lots of Scripture and made a pact with his buddies to spend his life as a warrior for Christ only to become deeply disillusioned when he found out how hard it is to be a full-out Christian. It was like he had passed basic training in the military, then was surprised on the battlefield when the enemy returned fire with real bullets. When this man fell down a couple of times he concluded, "It doesn't work." He abandoned hearty, passionate Christianity for a half-hearted imitation of "Telly Monster" from Sesame Street. This is a melancholy Christianity where folks wring their hands and the pure fire of the Holy Spirit is undermined by fear, indecision, frustration, and cynicism has become in vogue.

On the other side is the brand of Christianity offering positive mental attitude where a relationship with God is defined by the splendor of the arts, use of technology, the natural charisma of the preacher, and hearing a litany of thought-provoking, well-crafted messages. Polished packaging replaces spiritual weapons with which to fight the devil. This kind of experience builds self-esteem without offering Holy Spirit-empowered relief from destructive demons and familial, cultural, and personal sin. Worship in some cases becomes more a sensual theatrical experience rather than an encounter with the living Jesus.

WWJS – What Would Jesus Say?

Jesus was crystal clear in His teaching of the Kingdom of God as a mustard seed. He promises that although it begins small—crusty and unassuming—it will grow over time to be the greatest tree in the garden. So then, like all of God's living creation, the Kingdom of God is organic: farm work not factory work. One does not change during a summer of memorizing Bible verses or sitting through a thousand great messages, but throughout a lifetime of pushing up through the dirt, challenging sin, reaching always toward the Son, enduring long seasons of hot, cold, rain, and drought, and submitting one's self to the Father. The Holy Spirit is central to this process and the gift of tongues is a critical tool. Christianity is spiritual business requiring supernatural power, sustained faith, hope, and love. None of these ingredients can ever be neglected if God's people are to overcome.

What is Your Name?

Have you heard the story of Chris McCandless who, after graduating college, gave his money away, changed his name, abandoned his family, and took up the life of a tramp? He died in the wilderness of Alaska at twenty-four years old. Rising to the ranks of a folk hero, much has been written about him and a movie has been produced about his life. Most insightful for our purpose is his name change. Having been heavily influenced by Jack London, Leo Tolstoy, W. H. Davies and Henry David Thoreau, Chris McCandless hated materialism and traditional social order adopting the moniker Alexander Supertramp in his travels. (Supertramp is from the title of a work by Davies.)

He graduated from Emory University in 1990. From the moment of his departure after graduation until his death in August, 1992, he abandoned his family and traveled throughout the western U.S. where he met many people, always introducing himself as Alexander or Alex Supertramp. The people he met along the way liked him almost universally, with his intelligent mind and his well-bred way, but he never spoke of his past or revealed his real name. For the swan song of his odyssey, he decided to fulfill his dream of spending a summer in the wilderness of Alaska, living off the land far from the madding crowds. He hitched a ride from Fairbanks to a place in the region of Denali National Park and entered the Alaskan bush on April 28, 1992. In early September of that same year, a hunter discovered his body weighing just 67 lbs. He had been dead approximately two weeks, apparently from starvation.

Close to death, he left a note attached to the abandoned bus he had been using for shelter. It said,

"S.O.S. I need your help. I am injured, near death, and too weak to hike out. I am all alone, this is no joke. In the name of God, please remain to save me. I am out collecting berries close by and shall return this evening. Thank you, Chris McCandless. August?"

Notice the name. After over two years of denying his given name, when he was finally stripped of all the false idealism and his invented super-self failed, he was just plain old Chris McCandless. At the point of desperation and willing to beg to be saved, he finally came to terms with his name.

The same thing happened to the biblical character, Jacob. This trickster had to be stuck between a rock and a hard place before he would finally admit his name. Only after coming to terms with his most unlovely nature—supplanter, trickster, and usurper, could he become "Prince of God."

On one side we have believers who are resolved to their name, Jacob the imperfect—disillusioned and unwilling to fight to become Prince of God. On the other side are those who, like Alexander Supertramp, call themselves Prince of God, but do not limp because they have simply hung a new name tag on an old person and are frankly powerless to change themselves on the inside. These have crafted their Christianity like the Titanic, living in the comfort of popularity and technology but surprisingly vulnerable to the veritable icebergs of life.

We must embrace the true transformational power of God's Kingdom—the Holy Spirit. Specifically, we'll consider the place of the Holy Spirit's "gift of tongues" as a devotional tool for bringing the Holy Spirit to bear on our own lives, in our churches, and in the world at large. The intentional investment of quality time in spiritual prayer as a core practice is the missing

> *We must embrace the true transformational power of God's Kingdom— the Holy Spirit.*

power of the Church. I pray you are provoked.

Bob Engelhardt
Catskill Mountains, NY - 2012

5

Chapter One

THE HAMMER IN YOUR SPIRITUAL TOOLBOX

You want to pray in tongues. You may not know it yet, but when you are finished reading this book you will. In fact, you will never feel awkward again when discussing the gift of tongues. You will "get it." You will understand the purpose behind a God-given language you speak but do not understand. You will see that devotionally praying in tongues divides light from darkness in your inner life, sends angels off to work, illuminates Scripture, releases rivers of living water, and brings fantastic blessings throughout your life.

You will also see that the gift of tongues is not some circus sideshow or a strange lapse in God's good judgment. It is a vital, central weapon in the arsenal provided to battle darkness. Finally, you will learn it is good to desire the gift of tongues if you don't have it and super-cool to pray in tongues if you do. Most of all this is going to be great fun!

In the past thirty years I've had a blast serving Jesus and praying in tongues. I first came into the Kingdom in 1982 as the surprise recipient of a very dramatic conversion. This experience included a powerful baptism in the Holy Ghost with the gift of tongues gushing from inside and the Holy Spirit igniting my body and soul with pure holy fire! Convinced by great teachers early on of the importance of these tongues as a devotional tool, I have continued to value praying in the Spirit, logging many thousands of hours over the years. But for a long time, in my mind, the subject of tongues lacked something. I never saw a harmonious indication of the purpose of tongues in the overall flow of Old or New Testament. I felt the teaching was incomplete. Tongues always felt like a biblical anomaly.

What follows is a lens of understanding, which fills in the biblical blanks and shows the gift of tongues and their devotional use as part of God's master plan from the beginning. The gift of tongues is not only wonderful to receive but a central theme, clearly revealed throughout Scripture. And now, practically, on a personal level, speaking in tongues devotionally will change everything in your life for good!

Through this journey you will discover that the gift of tongues is the original super-power. It is a top-secret clandestine code language given by God to His earthly CIA agents. To use another metaphor, the gift of tongues is the hammer in the spiritual carpenter's toolbox. It is not the only tool by far, but one that is core to the process. As you read this book, the gift of tongues will be demystified and you will see the clear benefit in its devotional use—not de-spiritualized, but thoroughly demystified.

I think it is important to note I am not taking away from any sound biblical teaching, doctrine, responsibility, or practice. I am a church-loving, traditional evangelical, Bible-believing, charismatic Christian. Balance is key, but illumination should never be resisted. Therefore, let's go on a journey together and discover the hidden transformational power of God's Kingdom—*the devotional use of the gift of tongues.* The intentional investment of quality time in spiritual prayer as a core practice is a great resource.

Balance is key, but illumination should never be resisted.

Tongues: A Foundational Tool

The gift of tongues is a foundational tool of the Church. It is the on-switch of the portal to Heaven. It is the surprise super-power given by the risen King Jesus himself as a first order of business when He took His throne in Heaven (Acts 1 and 2).

Embedded in images and foreshadowed throughout the Old Testament, prophesied by Jesus and taught plainly by

Paul, meaning and depth shine from Scripture regarding this marvelous uniquely spiritual gift. We will consider many of these biblical accounts here because ultimately the devotional use of tongues is like a magical key providing access to certain important doors within an unseen kingdom.

In a mythical quest, the knight must discover many pieces to be fully equipped to finally defeat the dragon. Even so the gift of tongues is absolutely vital to perform certain spiritual duties. On our present day quest to defeat Satan, the great dragon of old, the gift of tongues opens specific spiritual doors. It heightens discernment, increases supernatural blessing, protection, growth, and awareness of the miraculous.

Some of God's plans are really unusual or mysterious. I mean, leave it to Almighty God to come up with the gift of tongues—a language spoken but not understood. No wonder it is such a controversial subject, especially in our analytical, scientific western culture. Truth is, we humans have difficulty wrapping our minds around a power that does not require our help other than using our voice to mutter gibberish—how embarrassing!

On top of this, even though some people receive profound experiences of baptism in the Holy Spirit, which frequently includes the gift of tongues, the ongoing practice of praying in tongues does not feel even remotely spiritual. It doesn't directly seem to make one smart, wise, or strong. Therefore, as time goes on, the initial infatuation of a cool new blessing from God wears off. It doesn't *seem* practical or productive. Most find it simply too boring or embarrassing to maintain the practice. Praying in tongues really challenges our prewired logic.

The purpose of this book is to ignite passion for the devotional exercise of tongues by illuminating the many blessings and benefits promised through Scripture. By the end you will know for sure that the gift of tongues, when practiced devotionally, is a gift from Heaven that can revolutionize your life in the most wonderful way!

It takes unwavering faith in Scripture to practice praying in tongues as a spiritual devotion and patience to realize the long-term benefit.

> *It takes unwavering faith in Scripture to practice praying in tongues as a spiritual devotion.*

Why Are Tongues a Problem?

From the outside speaking in tongues looks like pretty bizarre behavior. Even for those who have tongues, there doesn't seem like much benefit in using them that is not already included in our salvation package. Just as hearing someone speak an unknown foreign language is confusing, this is even more so when it is coming from our own mouths. It seems made up, or pretend. Our westernized cynical selves deeply fear being duped into practicing some ignorant religious party trick. The result is a tendency to smother enthusiasm for tongues.

The good news is this: Those who trust the Scripture enough to build a faith momentum for sustained regular devotional use of praying in tongues are among the richest and most well-rewarded of all believers!

Another pressure against praying in the Spirit as a devotional tool comes from Christians who are theologically predisposed against tongues for today. For the one trying to pray in the Spirit regularly, doubt seeps in when opposing voices begin to erode the faith imparted by good Spirit-filled Bible teaching and the initial enthusiasm of receiving the gift. This is the main point of this book: to help you sustain faith so you might receive the fullness of God's abundant blessing available through praying in tongues.

It is hard to accept something when you already believe something opposite to be true. This is the case for those who still refuse to embrace the restoration of the gifts of the Spirit. These well-intentioned folks are like the Pharisees criticizing Jesus when He healed the man with the withered hand on the Sabbath (Mark 3). The truth can be looking you in the face, but it is impossible to have an open heart when your mind is full. Jesus will reveal all things in His time.

The gift of tongues, like all of God's blessings, should be sought with a humble and faith-filled heart.

The gift of tongues, like all of God's blessings, should be sought with a humble and faith-filled heart. Joel prophesied that in the last days God's Spirit would be poured out on "all flesh" (see Joel 2 and Acts 2). The Holy Spirit's infilling is not arbitrary—it is like the sunshine—God's Spirit will fill all who open their hearts and seek.

In no way am I saying every church service should be a showcase of the gift of tongues. The gift of tongues is not meant to be a litmus test for salvation. Salvation comes through faith in Christ alone. Paul was very clear in 1 Corinthians 14, advising that church to back off in the use of tongues as a public proclamation gift in church services. But in that same passage he emphasizes his desire for all to speak in tongues and reveals that he does so more than anyone in their church—albeit privately.

Get it? Tongues are mainly for private devotional practice not public proclamation. It is incumbent upon believers, therefore, to embrace a culture where the fullness of the Holy Spirit is desired and the devotional use of tongues is valued as an ongoing lifelong spiritual discipline.

Why Not?

Before we begin considering the benefits of praying in tongues, an unspoken but glaringly obvious question needs to be asked: Why not pray in tongues as a devotional practice? Just on the surface the gift of tongues is:

* Promised by Jesus (Mark 16:17).
* A genuine supernatural sign that came with the Holy Spirit (Acts 2:4).
* A secret code language from God (Acts 2:4, 1 Corinthians 14:2).
* The language of angels (1 Corinthians 13:1).

* The Holy Spirit making prayers for us (Romans 8:26).
* Building up the one praying (1 Corinthians 14:4).
* Our spirit praying (1 Corinthians 14:14).
* Enthusiastically endorsed and exercised by Paul (1 Corinthians 14:5, 18).
* Joyfully received by believers in the book of Acts (2:4, 10:46, 19:6).

...and restored for us to utilize in the present day church.

So again, why not?

* Why would any believer not allow the Holy Spirit to access their tongue for Heaven's own purposes? What an amazing privilege!
* How crazy is it that Jesus died on the Cross, rose from the dead, ascended to Heaven and sent ... tongues?
* Tongues represent the power of God to do His own business in His own language. Where is the gratefulness? Where is the enthusiasm? Where are the modern-day Pauls? Where is our faith?

SIGNPOST

Having been raised in a main-line denomination, I remember going to a charismatic church service for the first time as a teenager around the mid nineteen-seventies and thinking the odd language I heard everyone speaking was most likely Spanish.

14

This put the gift of tongues on my radar. Then, shortly after we married, my wife Nancy received the baptism in the Holy Spirit and did her best to explain to me that tongues is a prayer language from God and people do not know what they are saying. I was curious about tongues but the subject seemed completely foreign to my mind and unapproachable to my reasoning.

In late November of 1982, after years of wondering, I finally asked Jesus to baptize me in the Holy Spirit with the gift of tongues. Late on a Sunday evening, I drove to the printing plant where I worked as manager by day. Knowing this time of night the place was empty, I had determined to secretly pray for the Holy Spirit and hope for the best. It is difficult to describe the fear I had when asking for a direct response from God, but it was palpable. I was embarrassed someone might hear me praying and I suppose I was also afraid God wouldn't answer.

When I arrived at the plant, I went down to the basement pressroom. After neurotically double-checking that I was there alone, I paced back and forth for a few minutes, trying to stir up enough courage to start. Finally I knelt on a wooden pallet and very tentatively said, "God ... Jesus ... Will you please come to me, fill me with the Holy Spirit, and give me the gift of tongues?" I specifically prayed this way because I thought of the gift of tongues as a sign of God's acceptance.

As the words were coming out of my mouth, I began to feel a strange tingling sensation on top of my head. Startled, I sprang off the pallet and frantically ran to the other side of the pressroom. Never having experienced anything even remotely supernatural before, I was terrified at the presence I felt. Something over there touched me! Something I couldn't see!

After a minute, I primed my courage a second time and decided to go back and see it through. I went to the same pallet, knelt in the same way and tried to recite exactly the same words. (I had already started a new religion!) I said, "God ... Jesus ... Will you please come to me, fill me with the Holy Spirit, and give me the gift of tongues?" This time when the tingling sensation started, I didn't move. It increased in intensity and swept over my body.

Some have described this feeling like that of warm honey or oil being poured over you. These descriptions are true. I was swept from head to toe with the most wonderful, warm, pure, and ecstatic feeling I had ever experienced. At the same time, I felt a pressure *pushing up from the inside of me and knew it must be the gift of tongues. I opened my mouth and began to speak as a beautiful new language literally gushed from inside of me.*

My speech faculties took on a life of their own as my voice continued to surge like a fire hydrant with exotic sounds and I experienced wave after wave of God's love. In fact, the tongues continuously poured with such intensity that for several minutes I honestly could not stop speaking this incredible articulate language containing distinct syllables, words, and phrases, all coming out of my mouth but which I could not understand.

I was so happy that I jumped and skipped like a little kid, running to a mirror and watching my own mouth talking with this foreign new God-language. I laughed and felt my chin and lips as these cool sounds, which did not originate in my mind, poured out. All of this was accompanied with a sense of joy. It seemed like every negative thing in me was simply gone. All the self-loathing, guilt, shame, and years of accumulated burdens instantly vanished like an overturned death sentence. I felt like an untethered helium balloon.

But the greatest thing of all was the knowledge that Jesus loved me! I felt so special! I was instantly an insider with God! I felt reborn! I was possessed with a profound sense of what I later learned that the Apostle Paul said, "If God is for me, who can be against me?" In that instant in time I didn't have any more problems, worries, or cares beyond the warmth of being in Him. I was forgiven—free and filled with happiness!

I associate my story with my first trip to Seattle, Washington, and how overwhelmed I was at the beauty of Mt. Rainier. Rising over fourteen thousand feet into the sky, this snow-capped peak is a magnificent spectacle of God's handiwork. The day I arrived the sky was blue and the majestic Mt. Rainier dominated the scenery, I could not take my eyes off it. Its beauty seemed to connect deeply with my soul.

As night fell that first evening, I was already looking forward to enjoying the same spectacular view for the next few days. I was disappointed in the morning to find that Seattle's famous rains had moved in during the night and low clouds and fog obstructed the view. So completely was Mt. Rainier cloaked that you would never guess in a million years behind the flat gray sky stood a dominating masterpiece of God's creation. I never got to see the mountain again on that trip, but I know what I saw.

That is exactly how I know the gift of tongues comes directly from Jesus. People can argue interpretation and doctrine. They can believe or not believe. They can theorize, theologize, and speculate, but the vast majorities are doing so from the fog. I know differently. Tongues are not a biblical quirk; they are a portal to eternity.

Tongues are not a biblical quirk; they are a portal to eternity.

You see, I've seen Mt. Rainier for myself. I know it is there so it doesn't matter what anyone else says. It is the same way I've experienced God in the depth of my being and gushing forth in new tongues. I called Him, He answered in a way more tangible than my eyewitness of that great mountain and at the same time Jesus slipped me His cell number: the gift of tongues.

I know Jesus Christ personally. I've met Him. I'm family. I speak in the family tongue. Having been touched by Him on the inside, I am left with a residue of His presence. So now, when I read the Bible I recognize the same Spirit as the One who touched me that day. Men can argue over tongues, whether they believe or not, but I know it's true. I received my prayer language from Jesus himself, and we keep in touch.

19

I know most people do not receive the gift of tongues with this type of extraordinary spiritual fanfare. I do not consider myself to be in any way better than those who humbly receive tongues through faith and perseverance. God met me in a unique and special way. The main benefit I obtained because of my extraordinary experience has been a deep desire to understand tongues more.

Portal to Heaven

Genesis 11 describes the Tower of Babel where God came down and found a civilization determined to work together in order to make themselves great—but not through Him. Their plan was to build a city on the plain of Shinar including a tower whose top would reach into Heaven. In essence, they wanted to penetrate the higher powers of both Heaven and Earth for human greatness and social benefit. In response to their rebellious stand, God cursed their language, breaking communication between people. This ruined their plans and drove them apart, causing them to migrate throughout the world.

On Pentecost, in pure prophetic reversal of Babel, when God drew to himself a humble and prayerful people in one accord in Acts 2, He also altered their language. In this case, when God came down and the disciples spoke in tongues as the Spirit gave utterance, instead of misunderstanding one another, people from many nations heard them speaking in their own native languages.

,Pentecost reversed Babel. In both cases—the curse and the blessing—language alterations are the common theme. This shows that the gift of tongues is necessary to the coming of God's Kingdom.

The Tower of Babel was man's attempt to access higher things by human genius and social collective consciousness apart from God. The gift of tongues, on the other hand, is a tactic of God to unite His beloved. At Babel, God created confusion of language and therefore disunity, but the new tongues given at Pentecost came to produce understanding among God's people. Praying in tongues, therefore, is a language of unity and submission to God's wisdom over human innovation.

If the following statement was true for the rebellious people of Babel, how much more shall it be true for God's own? "The people are one and they all have one language, and this is what they begin to do; now nothing that they propose to do will be withheld from them" (Genesis 11:6, NKJV). This Scripture holds echoes of Jesus' words: "If you can believe, all things are possible to him who believes" (Mark 9:23, NKJV).

The miracle of Pentecost turns the Tower of Babel on its head. On the Plain of Shinar men elevated themselves in rebellion to God. On Pentecost, God sent His Spirit down through a tower—a portal of His own design. Common to both stories is new tongues. At Babel, the new tongues from God drove people apart. On Pentecost, seemingly unintelligible tongues were perfectly understood by people of many diverse human languages. The conclusion must be that this language gift upon the newly birthed Church would somehow draw God's people into perfect unity, a prerequisite for Jesus coming again. The correlation cannot be denied.

Come along with me on a journey into the supernatural and discover the great mystery—hidden in plain view— embedded clearly in the Word of God. I promise you will receive insight into a wild ride of God's constant companionship and continual blessings!

Ask Yourself

* Am I open to a broader understanding of the purpose of speaking in tongues?
* Am I willing to believe that God would use me beyond my previous expectations?
* Am I open to God praying through me?
* What's most difficult for me in surrendering my tongue, language, and communication completely to God's use?

Chapter Two

PRACTICE REVEALS PURPOSE

*You did not choose Me, but I chose you and
appointed you that you should go and bear fruit,
and that your fruit should remain, that whatever you
ask the Father in My name He may give you.*

John 15:16

SIGNPOST

*About five years into my walk with the Lord I was
driving along one day, singing and praising God. I
was on Sandy Plains Road, a familiar small back road
in the Greene County township of Cairo, New York,
in the privacy of my car just enjoying the Lord. As
usual, I was jumping back and forth between singing*

in the Spirit and alternating with familiar praise choruses in English. It was mid-afternoon and I was feeling good, loving God with both my mouth and heart, singing at full volume to the only audience (besides me) who really enjoys my singing voice—Jesus! (Actually, the only place I've ever been asked to lead worship singing was while doing prison ministry in a maximum-security prison ... and they didn't like it. So I keep my really good stuff for the car!)

Anyway, I was driving westward on this back road and came to a place where the dense forested area ends, opening into a beautiful vista of the Catskill Mountain range. Having grown up in the Hudson Valley, the ever-changing hues of blue, purple, green, and gray of the Catskills with their distinct outline against the sky was a treat for the eye on any occasion, but this day something different happened. The mountains lit up! Suddenly, like a child's illuminated bedroom nightlight, the entire vista radiated a luminescence that was absolutely a supernatural experience. I don't know how else to describe it but that it seemed to be glowing. But not like a soft light, more like a blazing LED billboard. And it wasn't a cold impersonal light; it was somehow full of life. It was glowing with vibrant, radiant, living light.

This unsolicited experience had such an effect on me that I spontaneously gushed with praise, joy, and gratitude.

I had a feeling that the angels must have just lifted for a moment the shroud of spiritual blindness on me and showed me a glimmer of creation as God sees it—full of His glory. At that moment I knew God's glory saturates everything, everywhere, all the time!

What I did not understand for several more years was the prophetic importance of the experience. As it would turn out, my destiny in God had everything to do with this vision when, several years later, I was offered to take the leadership of a small church-plant in Margaretville, New York, a community of 630 residents in the rural heart of the Catskill Mountains. Like Paul's Macedonian call and Abraham's call out of his father's country into a new land God had set aside for him, in the years to come I would become the pastor of a small church in the Catskills and it would grow over time into a regional powerhouse of influence radiating God's love and light. This vision was granted to me as I prayed in the Spirit—as I exercised the gift of tongues devotionally. One of the great benefits of praying in tongues as a devotional practice is the increase of spiritual intuition.

One of the great benefits of praying in tongues as a devotional practice is the increase of spiritual intuition.

The question that inevitably meets you at the door to a discussion about the gift of tongues is: *Can or should everyone pray in tongues?* The short answer is I don't really know, and the long answer is for another book. I believe the gift of tongues is a central piece of gear without which God's army will never accomplish its mission. Speaking in tongues is not a litmus test for salvation, but that doesn't diminish its importance. This contribution is meant to describe components of the spiritual playing field where tongues are concerned. It is written for the purpose of encouraging the devotional use of tongues and perhaps to stimulate a desire for others to seek the gift for the first time.

Flow in Tongues Continually

I would like to present a compelling argument for the regular devotional use of tongues in a practical sense.

Much good work has been written over the years on the subject of the Holy Spirit and the gift of tongues. However, the contribution along with urgent appeal I would like to present is a compelling argument for the regular devotional use of tongues in a practical sense.

Most people who have the gift of tongues, sadly, do not pray in tongues very much. Unfortunately it has become a "been there, done that" element of faith for most. For me, since being baptized in the Holy Spirit thirty years ago, I have continued to pray in tongues devotionally and deeply believe it is a mandatory strategic element in the coming of the Kingdom.

As a product of the tail end of the charismatic movement, which is regarded by many to be among the greatest moves of God in the history of the Church, my love for praying in tongues was initially ignited by the sovereign manner in which I received the gift.

I remember my first lucid thought in relationship to the use of tongues after being filled with the Holy Spirit. I said to myself in pondering my new ability, *If my dad gave me a bicycle as a birthday present, he would be happy to see me riding that new bike all the time. He'd smile when he got home from work each day and I was enjoying my gift from him because he picked it out for me. He'd be gratified because the bike cost him something and his boy really appreciated it and used it to the fullest. He would feel like it was money well spent.*

On the other hand, if I asked my dad for a new bike and he bought it for me and then I never rode it but instead threw it in the bushes to rust, he would regret spending his hard earned money for my gift. Although he would still love me, he would be disappointed with me and sorry to have believed me. That's how I felt about the gift of tongues—and I still do. Jesus gave His life (at least in part) to buy the gift of tongues for His Church and I want to make my Father glad. Besides, not knowing any better at the time, I figured every Spirit-filled Christian must pray in tongues a lot and I had a bunch of catching up to do. It wasn't until quite a few years later that I began to feel something like the

WWII Japanese soldier on a remote Pacific island, still fighting the war thirty years after his countrymen had surrendered.

I remember as a kid one year begging my parents for an electric guitar for my birthday. The Monkees were all the rage on television and radio in 1966-67, and turning ten years old I could see myself being the coolest rock n' roll guy ever. I pulled out all the stops with my folks. Like Ralphie from *A Christmas Story*, I pled my case with the passion of a tort lawyer and all the earnestness of Mother Teresa. "If I get this guitar," I promised, "I give my word to practice it for hours each day. I will do better in school, stop fighting with my brothers, take the garbage out for the rest of my life," ... and whatever else I could come up with to move my parents' hearts. I suddenly began to sing with my cool-guy voice around the house and took up air-guitar. I knew it was a long shot but I had to go for it.

This beautiful guitar, the object of my affection, was hanging in the Jamesway Discount Department Store in the village of Catskill, NY. The price tag was $19.99. Twenty bucks looks laughable now, but in those days with seven kids and one blue-collar income that was a lot of dough—far more than usual birthday present budget. But glory hallelujah! It worked! I broke them down! I won the battle!

At my birthday party, as soon as I saw the triangular shaped box, I couldn't tear through the wrapping paper fast enough. In my imagination I had already played concerts at Shea Stadium with this baby; my dream had come true. "Come to daddy!" As I opened the lid, there it was—too beautiful to imagine. I picked it up, positioned it with my coolest rock guy pose, and took my very first strum—oddly, though it made a noise, for some reason it wasn't music. In fact it didn't sound anything like music. Not a trace of the Monkees or the Beatles or even boring old-person music.

I mean, I knew theoretically it took a little practice to play the guitar and I would have to take lessons, but something must be wrong—it shouldn't sound *that* bad. The music was inside of me. I could feel it. But it wouldn't come out. *What gives?* I thought. Again, strummmm—whatever that gross sound was, it wasn't music. Truth was, the imagination of the gift was better than the gift. I think it's important to say in my defense that we didn't have anyone who played an instrument in our family, so my parents could offer little help and the anticlimax of the new guitar was probably predictable.

I did go on to learn how to pluck the Monkees' song, "Steppin' Stone" on one string and took lessons from Mr. Esposito every Saturday for a while. In my defense, Mr. Esposito was in his eighties, smoked a great big disgusting cigar, and wanted me to play "On Top of Old Smoky." (Reminds me of some churches I've been to.) All I wanted to know was, "WHEN AM I GOING TO SOUND LIKE THE MONKEES?" I never did get to sound like the Monkees or anyone else remotely cool, but the guitar looked very sharp propped up in the corner of my room.

That's the gift of tongues to most Spirit-filled believers. It's a conquest. It is a trophy propped up in the corner of the room. It is something that once obtained goes unused, becomes dusty and would make no difference if it were there or not. Just like a guitar requires a framework of instruction, understanding, discipline, patience, and practice to make beautiful music, the gift of tongues is but a dissonant strum without understanding and investment. The gift of tongues must be practiced devotedly in order for its ongoing spiritual benefits to be experienced continually in the life of the believer.

In this book we are going to consider a number of elements of tongues that will begin to bring the knowledge, skill, and harmony necessary for making music. Some of those elements are:

1. A foreshadow of tongues found in Genesis 1.
2. Praying in tongues separates light from darkness or creates spiritual contrast.
3. Praying in tongues brings angels.
4. Praying in tongues brings revelation.

Ask Yourself

* Am I willing to receive something from God over which I have no say or control?
* Am I willing to discipline myself to be open to God's Spirit and the gift of tongues even if I do not quickly benefit?
* Am I willing to submit my reason to the "mind of Christ"?

Chapter Three

BLUEPRINT FOR OUR CONGREGATION

Ask, and it will be given to you; seek, and you will find; knock, and it will be opened to you. For everyone who asks receives, and he who seeks finds, and to him who knocks it will be opened.

Matthew 7:7-8

SIGNPOST

In August 1991, I took the pastorate of a small rural church plant. Chartered in the late 1980s as Christ Community Church, it was located in the Village of Margaretville, New York, population 630. The founder had begun the work ten years earlier as a home fellowship and moved around the community to various locations over the years. When I took the helm from him, there were just a few families in attendance. A former beer and beverage discount store three miles from the village proper had just been purchased by the church and renovated to provide a sixty-seat sanctuary and Sunday school room.

The church took off immediately growing significantly even as I continued employment as a printer, working full time, twelve-hour night shifts for a company an hour's drive away. After a solid year of increased attendances it seemed the church growth was going to continue indefinitely. Excited, I took a leap of faith leaving my printing job. Unfortunately the growth soon after tapered off and we hit a frustrating attendance plateau. Another year later I had to go back to the printing plant and work outside the church full-time for two more years.

As difficult times tend to do to me, I responded by increasing my prayer life, seeking the Lord for a breakthrough as pressure mounted. Since meeting the Lord I have always been confident that His plan for me is good success. I have never been bogged down with a theological crisis that says God prefers tiny churches. It seems to me that God is all about numbers—like 3,000 getting saved on the day of Pentecost. So the stalled financial and numerical growth of Christ Community

Church drove me to even more prayer in the Spirit. In a crisis, an hour a day is never enough praying in tongues. Crisis challenges believers to up the ante.

One day in the deep of the winter of early 1995, I was praying in our humble, unheated sanctuary. Actually it was equipped with electric baseboard heat, but we couldn't afford to turn it on except for services. It was every bit as cold inside as it was outside—below twenty degrees Fahrenheit. I distinctly remember the frozen breath vapor billowing as I walked in circles praying in the Spirit; walking and praying. One funny thing about getting a visitation from God, you tend to remember the smallest details. I remember like it was yesterday the lined winter boots, blue parka jacket with a snorkel hood, and the breath vapor fogging my glasses if I breathed wrong.

Suddenly, in one single package of thought, my mind was illuminated with the headline: Catskill Mountain Christian Center. Most uncannily about this thought is that it descended on my mind instantly containing the entire picture of the future and destiny of our ministry. I literally ran, got a pen and paper, and wrote down every detail of the vision as it was given to me. The entire picture came in one complex deposit. Within a year we officially changed the name of the church and started to build according to the blueprint. We overcame our growth plateau and an amazing new season of vision, enrichment, and productivity was born which elevated immeasurably and permanently the self-image of the church.

Did you notice in the SIGNPOST section what I wrote as a benefit of tongues? I wrote, "...my mind was illuminated." Illumination by the Spirit speaks of a light coming into darkness even as the Incarnate Word, Jesus Christ, was light coming into darkness and the darkness wasn't able to overcome the light (John 1). Illumination coming through the gift of tongues may be depicted as a match lighting a candle. The candle (you or me) has the created potential to bring light with all its benefits—to illuminate a dark problem or cloudy understanding with spiritual intuition. So the fire of the Spirit's tongues (Acts 2) falls upon the believer and illumines the moment granting the mind (*nous*) wisdom, knowledge, and understanding (Isaiah 11:1-2). So the simple yet profound insight of the name and picture of the church was given to me by the Spirit as I prayed in tongues.

I have learned that if God gives the vision, God will fulfill the vision. The price of a God-given vision: prayer in the Spirit. If you sow to the Spirit you will reap from the Spirit. A God-given vision gives a perfect and pure channel of faith to exercise and proclaim, knowing that God will do what He says He will do. Most amazing is that right now (seventeen years later) nearly every facet of the vision has been fulfilled in a more spectacular way than I could have imagined. The few points yet to be fulfilled are still actively in process or on the top of the "things to do" list.

Drinking of Jesus

On the last day, that great day of the feast, Jesus stood and cried out, saying, 'If anyone thirsts, let him come to Me and drink. He who believes in Me, as the Scripture has said, out of his heart will flow rivers of living water.' But this He spoke concerning the Spirit, whom those believing in Him would receive; for the Holy Spirit was not yet given, because Jesus was not yet glorified.

John 7:37-39

In this passage, Jesus says that if we'll do something, He'll do something. He requires something of us and promises something from Him. *"If anyone thirsts let him come to Me and drink."* Required of us is that we drink of Jesus. What does it mean to drink of Jesus? Simply put it means internalizing Him: His actions and words. It means allowing His words to pierce us, change us, empower us, and inspire us. It means learning to love Him, and working His Word like an internal Rubik's Cube trying to align all of the sides to understand and conform to His excellent ways. It means stretching to believe everything He said is the absolute truth.

"Drinking from Jesus" means wrestling Him for His promises and blessings. It means looking through Jesus Christ as a lens to understand life. It means looking through Him backward to understand the Old Testament and looking through Him forward to understand Acts and the Epistles. It means coming to terms with the world around us: history, the church, political systems, science, religion, philosophy, family, and education. It means understanding that at the end of all things Jesus Christ is the only lens which will align truth as it should be. This is coming to Jesus to drink. In drinking from Jesus, we learn as the disciples did on the way to Emmaus that only He washes away the dust from our eyes and gives us full vision of Him in all of Scripture.

Unfortunately, humans tend too often to find some kind of compromised position between pure faith and acceptable modern knowledge. They develop comfortable theologies that are more functional than truly spiritual. Jesus said essentially, "If you come to Me; if you're thirsty and drink, then out of your belly—your innermost being—will flow rivers of living water." Sort of sounds like the old Mentos in a bottle of Diet Coke trick. If I come to Jesus and drink from Him, rivers of living water erupt and flow from inside. Wow! Internalize Jesus (believe in, trust, study, and deeply consider) and the Holy Spirit will flow from inside of my body! Here we see cause and effect—two separate operations—a "Jesus Mento" is dropped in my system and rivers of living water flow out of my innermost being. Again, this is two separate operations with the context explicitly being that He was speaking of the Holy Spirit.

To drink of Christ speaks of us as empty vessels

needing to be filled with something or someone other than ourselves. We can be filled with the noise of cable news chatter or radio music. We can listen to our devices or continually read texts and emails. Such fast food diets rarely satisfy for more than a moment. What fills you? In your emptiness, how are you comforted or satisfied? I know at times when I am thirsty, I can drink volumes of soda without quenching my thirst. Then I down a glass of cool, refreshing water and my thirst vanishes. The same is true with the Spirit... drink Jesus and rivers of living water flow!

According to Jesus' words, the living, dynamic presence of river-like volumes of the Holy Spirit of God flowing should be an identifying characteristic of every believer. Furthermore, the Scripture relates that Jesus intentionally stood up, unsolicited, at the crescendo of the feast and cried the words out—very awkward! It is self-evident, therefore, that this is a stand-alone, urgent bulletin; a central eternal truth that all believers in all ages must stop their religious

According to Jesus' words, the living, dynamic presence of river-like volumes of the Holy Spirit of God flowing should be an identifying characteristic of every believer.

activities to consider. It is meant to jar us to our core. This is no peripheral doctrine! This is eternal truth, which must be understood, sought after, and embraced. No simple passing this one off to the Pentecostals.

Then what does it mean to have rivers of living water flowing from inside our innermost being? Does Jesus mean we should be quoting lots of Bible verses? (I seem to remember in the wilderness while tempting Jesus, the devil had pretty handy use of the Bible too.) Does Jesus mean we should speak only in a syrupy effeminate way that shows everyone how loving we are? Does He mean we copy some quirky sermon style in our speech and say "G'-loh-ree" with a long "O"? How can we know if rivers of living water are flowing from our innermost being?

I would offer that the gift of tongues is the only sure-fire way to know the Holy Spirit is flowing out from the inside. Every time, any place, any hour of the day, no matter how anointed you feel or don't feel, and under any internal or external circumstances, activating the gift of tongues unleashes the Holy Spirit—the rivers of living water—to flow from your innermost being. That is an absolute, every time, always, never fails, one hundred percent, guaranteed super-power.

Praying in tongues is the single most supernatural thing one will ever do continually in this life. Other supernatural gifts and events like healing, prophecy, wisdom, or knowledge may come and go intermittently as needed. But tongues is praying without ceasing. The believer can use this gift as much as he wants.

Praying in tongues is the single most supernatural thing one will ever do continually in this life.

It is not fattening or high in cholesterol. It won't rot your teeth or give you a communicable disease. It is allowing the free flow of the rivers of God to pour from within. So why such neglect?

As I've come to understand it over the years, a major problem with the devotional use of tongues is that the practitioner does not understand what they are saying and therefore become bored. Our Western culture's emphasis on mind over spirit, on reason over mystery, and on knowledge over relationship lock out the flow of God in and through us. So in praying by the Spirit, we are not invited by God to know what is being communicated though His own body. This makes spiritual praying a pure act of faith, of submission, of obedience, and surrender. The gift of tongues requires absolute blind trust to invest one's valuable (or expendable) time in praying in tongues.

The "ROI" (Return on Investment) comes to the Giver and returns to the investor abundantly—overflowing and completely mysteriously. As a gift, it cannot be earned or learned. It doesn't make you smart or give you good feelings. Nobody can tell if you have done it or not. It does not make you more artistic. It does not make you a better singer or increase your bank account. It does not save the unsaved, build a new church building, or guarantee success with your business deal. It is raw spiritual exercise done from the will not the feelings or intellect.

The tongues gift flows effortlessly as a discipline of grace. Just as air and breathing come naturally to the creature, so tongues come supernaturally to the believer—a new Spirit-filled creation in Christ Jesus. No, that's not an oxymoron. A discipline predisposes the disciple to receive whatever the Master gives, whenever given, and whatever the desire of the Master, not the disciple.

An Analogy with the Tree of Life

In the Garden of Eden, God made an arbitrary decision to withhold certain knowledge and Adam was not invited to eat of it. It was God's sovereign choice. At the same time, the Tree of Life was ostensibly perfectly accessible to Adam, but eating it only promised something called "life." He already had life and had never seen anything die before, so that tree must have seemed to him like the "Tree of Air" would seem to us. It promised him what he already had, just apparently more of it. How could he even have a concept of what death would be like?

To Adam, the Tree of Life offered no good feelings, no elevation of self, fulfilled no curiosity, and offered neither mind-blowing knowledge nor anything appealing to the eye. The Tree of Life only had value because God told him it did. It was purely an issue of faith. He very well may have planned on getting to eat from it sometime but with no immediate danger, there was certainly no rush. He could never have known how horrible death really was or how good life really is. Death was just an obscure theory to Adam.

The gift of tongues is imparted in much the same way.

Jesus clearly says that rivers of living water WILL flow out of the innermost beings of those who believe in Him and He was speaking of the Holy Spirit. So where are all the rivers? A trickle or two doesn't constitute rivers. The hindrance is that privately praying in tongues takes the same kind of faith as Adam needed to eat from the Tree of Life; there is no sensual, emotional, social, or intellectual fulfillment. At least when I pray in English I can engage my intellect—I can participate. But when I pray in tongues I just have to trust in rivers of living water to flow.

So why should I pray in tongues then? I've already got eternal life in Jesus. Isn't that enough? At least when praying in English I can recommend to God how He should order my universe, but praying in tongues leaves me out of the loop.

Adam is not inspired by the Tree of Life and, truthfully, he doesn't really get it. That other tree however was so cool, so relevant! That Tree of the Knowledge of Good and Evil looked awesome, was said to be delicious to the taste, and seemed to promise the taboo secrets of the universe. It provided the inside scoop—the dirt on both the good and the evil.

This is so much like the Church's treatment of the gift of tongues it's frightening. The great gift of God's Spirit, the very substance of eternal life flowing from our innermost being like rivers of living water is neglected. Ministry becomes a competition with people's physical senses, intellect, emotions, or *self*. Here's some news:

If you have a relationship with Jesus Christ, you already have all knowledge!

In conclusion, this is the problem with tongues. Because the Holy Spirit does not produce fruit quickly and is difficult to define, the mind becomes bored. However, like the balance of the many elements required for optimum physical health, spiritual praying is a vital element to overall spiritual wholeness. Eating good food is great, but without exercising, the body does not become fit or athletic. The same goes for your spirit. A believer who eats the Word of God but does not exercise the gift of tongues does not develop his own depth. Praying in the Holy Spirit releases the rivers of life. It does not edify intellect but rather the subconscious spirit and is a function of faith and trust in God's process, not one's personal abilities.

Ask Yourself

* When I cannot control something within me, how do I feel?
* What attracts me to what is known and visible over what is invisible and mysterious?
* What keeps the rivers of living waters from flowing out of me? (Check one or more that apply.)
    * ☐ Fear
    * ☐ Confusion
    * ☐ Doubt
    * ☐ Self-centeredness
* What will I do about whatever hinders the Spirit in my life?

ARE YOU SURE?

Now it came to pass in those days that He went out to the mountain to pray, and continued all night in prayer to God.

Luke 6:12

SIGNPOST

In the first few years after being filled with the Holy Spirit, I soaked up God's Word like a sponge and felt compelled from within to sprint forward in prayer, investing many hours in the Spirit. I was acutely aware that I had the love and attention of the Creator of the universe—the One who could do anything. At the center of it all, I was (and still am) head over heels in love with Jesus. Immediately after the Holy Spirit entered my body, the words of the Bible became alive to me. Previously, I found the Bible nearly impossible to read. The sentences never seemed to make much sense; the language was archaic and the thoughts did not really connect with anything that mattered. But after the Holy Spirit filled me, I found my mind, without effort, fascinated by the Scriptures and I could intrinsically sense a depth, power, and life in the words—especially Jesus' words!

Jesus' words became capsules filled with life, depth, mystery, and illumination. They seemed to literally jump off of the pages into my mind and heart and stayed there, working in me and changing my perspective on everything. I soon came to believe that there is a centrality and concentrated focus in Jesus' words and actions that become the lens for everything else in life. Everything is understood through Jesus Christ— His words and actions. If I read the Old Testament, it is through Jesus. If I read the New Testament epistles, it is through Jesus. If I learn science, philosophy, politics, psychology, sociology, anthropology, or any other "ology," it is through Jesus.

Jesus' earthly words will be the gauge by which all truth is judged.

Jesus said, "Heaven and earth will pass away, but My words will by no means pass away" (Matthew 24:35). This means that somehow throughout eternity, even in Heaven, like the plumb line in the hand of Zerubbabel (Zechariah 4:10), Jesus' earthly words will be the gauge by which all truth is judged. This became the central pursuit of my newly found walk with the Lord—discovering everything I could about Jesus. This nurtured a desire over time to also act like He acted and, as much as possible, do what He did.

At some point in the first couple of years, I began to desire to pray all night long like Jesus did (Luke 6:12). The problem with that simple little task, I would come to find out, is that Jesus set a pretty high bar for His followers and the old flesh likes to kick and scream in the process of being subjugated to the Holy Spirit! But I was determined to conform myself, as much as possible, to the Master's image, so I set a night to conquer this feat. At this point it was not uncommon for me to pray well past midnight each night, many times to one or even occasionally two o'clock in the morning, so I felt I was ready.

I picked a Friday night so it wouldn't affect my work and set out to undertake the Christ-like endeavor. Starting at about ten o'clock I prayed outside the house until eleven thirty or so and then I came into the kitchen, which, in those days, was my nighttime prayer closet. I walked in circles around our oak table praying in the Spirit and in English, praising, worshiping, and groping for a God who cannot be seen with the human eye. I desired to connect with Him in faith and to stretch my mind to stay alert to the process. One o'clock, one thirty, two o'clock, two fifteen, two thirty, quarter to three—somewhere around 3:00 a.m., I had a brilliant idea. I had seen godly people sometimes lying prostrate before the Lord and quickly concluded that I should exercise this great expression of humility. It's only right!

Sounds funny but the evil mind is always there to rationalize the comfort of the flesh and I was open to suggestions! I stretched out on my stomach on the hardwood floor determined to keep on praying through the night and the next thing I knew I was waking up and it was six in the morning.

Uncomfortable, filled with disgust at my own weakness and feeling like a Loser with a capital "L," I blurted out to the Lord, "Father, I'm so sorry. I just want to be like Jesus."

Immediately, like a blast furnace inside my mind, a voice came up from within, breaking in on my stream of consciousness, and said, "ARE YOU SURE?"

I did not really have to think about it but I just sort of knew if God was asking me it must be a pretty serious question. I said, "Yes Lord, with everything inside me."

A second time the furnace roared, "ARE YOU SURE?" "Yes Lord," I said. "It is the only thing I've ever really wanted."

A third time the voice blasted, "ARE YOU SURE?"

"Yes Lord. Absolutely. Yes. More than anything in the world, I just want to be like Jesus." Then the moment passed and God was silent, but since that experience I've always understood that this was the moment when God accepted my recruitment into His personal discipleship school.

In the beginning God created the heavens and the earth. The earth was without form, and void; and darkness was on the face of the deep. And the Spirit of God was hovering over the face of the waters.

Genesis 1:1-2

A Main Point of the Bible

Among other things, the Bible is a prophetic book written to reveal God to the seeker. Within its pages lie patterns and keys to unlock the secrets of the heavenly realm. Because God is infinitely deep and profound, the sincere student is sure to find treasure in the Word to enlighten himself and reveal insight allowing each generation to celebrate God anew. In the Book of the Revelation, the image of elders surrounding the throne of God represents the linear timeline of history as it exists all at once around His throne. As secrets are unlocked from the Scriptures, new facets of His glory dazzle the Church, causing the elders to fall down and cry out holy, holy, holy all over again in every generation. Understanding the gift of tongues is one fresh, new, dazzling facet of brilliant glory.

The Rainbow Connection

Musing about eternity and longing for what lies beyond, Kermit the Frog sings "Rainbow Connection" in 1979's, *The Muppet Movie*. Wikipedia says of the song by Kenneth Ascher and Paul Williams: "'Rainbow Connection' serves the same purpose in *The Muppet Movie* that 'Over the Rainbow' serves in *The Wizard of Oz* with nearly equal effectiveness: **an opening establishment of the characters' driving urge for something more in life.**"

It's actually more than that. The song resonated so well with audiences it was nominated for an Academy Award, not only because it's a beautiful song but also because it comes to us from Kermit—a representation of our better selves; a frog yearning for higher connection. It is, in fact, a poignant song that speaks wistfully of the deep unspoken universal feeling that we are estranged from an unknown homeland. It speaks of the human heart's cry for the connection we instinctively know is missing. *"Why are there so many songs about rainbows and what's on the other side... Someday we'll find it, the rainbow connection, the lovers, the dreamers and me."*

Deeper humans have sought for a missing *something* since our original banishment from Eden. Somewhere inside if we look really hard, we feel a subconscious melancholic mourning for what we've lost and can't find. We know we are higher creatures and feel incomplete but only get flashes and glimpses of the world that too often seems to be reserved for the lovers, the dreamers—and apparently, Kermit.

I knew a leak was sprung in the dam of that elusive place beyond the rainbow when I got the gift of tongues. It was my first taste of the supernatural world to come and boy, did it taste good! My unwavering commitment to a life of devotional praying in tongues therefore, has always

The greatest apostle of all time saw no sense in using tongues publicly for show, but privately it was his secret weapon!

flowed from a restless passion to break the rest of that dam down. The Apostle Paul knew tongues were a key to this place and fully maximized this gift in his devotional prayer time. The one who unashamedly prayed in tongues more than any in the Corinthian Church and maybe the greatest apostle of all time saw no sense in using tongues publicly for show, but privately it was his secret weapon!

Observation—Discovering the Spirit's Frequency

A breakthrough for me in trying to understand the Holy Spirit and tongues was John Wimber's book, *Power Healing*, which offers an intelligent and thoughtful treatment of the activity of the Holy Spirit in healing and the other gifts as well. I remember watching Wimber interviewed on Trinity Broadcasting Network (TBN) at the book's release (1987). He discussed his practice of setting up a clinical laboratory environment where he would teach people how to pray more effectively for healing. On TBN's "Praise the Lord" program, he showed such a lab demonstration presenting his technique. It was a real breakthrough for me and I quickly ran to my brother Chuck's Christian bookstore and bought a copy of *Power Healing*—to this day one of the most important books I've studied.

A point that stuck with me is that when praying over someone for healing it is important to pray with your eyes open because there are common physical phenomena accompanying the presence of the Holy Spirit. Among the specific symptoms he cited are fluttering eyelids and sometimes trembling by the person receiving prayer. This was really exciting to me because I too had noticed these common symptoms, but never heard them discussed in such a frank and natural manner. In the age of the larger-than-life platform preacher, the accessibility to the supernatural Wimber offered to a common seeker like me was exhilarating!

Filled with the Holy Ghost and praying in tongues devotionally for over five years at that point, I commonly saw fluttering eyelids when praying for people. Wimber demystified the phenomena and offered practical understanding for regular folks. The effect was to liberate me and many other believers to participate in the power of the Holy Spirit as a normal utility tool of Kingdom people. It was also during this time that I first consciously noted the similarity of these fluttering eyelids with the chattering rate of frequency when speaking in tongues. Like electricity coming from an AC (alternating current) outlet, the pulsation is strikingly similar.

The Tongues Connection

Next I noticed this "Alternating Current" trait is a common characteristic of the Holy Spirit's presence throughout the Bible.

1. The wings of the Holy Spirit in the form of a dove descending on Jesus fluttered. A dove is a small pigeon and its flight involves intense flapping of the wings. Still life paintings over the centuries have tended to depict a bird in a soaring position due to the limitations of the medium but there is no biblical evidence to support this. The description, "like a dove," reveals an intense

flapping sight and sound of the Spirit's presence descending on Jesus.

2. The Holy Ghost appearing as tongues of fire blown by a mighty wind in the second chapter of Acts fluttered. In the religious images of my youth the Holy Spirit on Pentecost was always depicted as docile candle-like, vertical flames upon each disciple's head. Again, the limits of ancient, still life artists have crept forward without updating the mental image. Obviously, the combination of tongues of fire and very strong wind necessitates the appearance being more like the fire coming from a blast furnace—flames intensely flapping and being blown sideways.

3. The disciples' tongues fluttered as the Spirit gave them utterance. As the spiritual tongues of fire lit upon the disciples, their tongues began to flutter with the same intense frequency as the Holy Spirit moved into their bodies. The tongues of fire are prophetically correlated with the tongues of the disciples. Same fluttering motion and similar flapping (chattering) sound.

4. *Young's Literal Translation* says of Genesis 1:2, *"Darkness is on the face of the deep, and the Spirit of God fluttering on the face of the waters"* (emphasis added). This connection is enormously important because it ties the observed fluttering characteristic of the Spirit of God in Genesis 1 with the gift of tongues.

So in short, Holy Spirit tongues correlates undeniably with the Spirit of God hovering, or moving (*fluttering*) in Genesis 1, which make them vital to God's creative work in human lives. Remember that when God's Spirit appears, the power of the progenitor manifests. God's Spirit births into being that which did

In the Creation, God's Spirit births into being that which did not exist.

not exist. So God's Spirit births into being all of creation in Genesis 1 and births the Church into being in Acts 2. That is why the very first order of business necessary for the Church to start in the upper room was tongues—the Spirit of God turbine could now go to work inside the power plant of human bodies. Through the Word of God and the moving Spirit released through the tongues of believers, God would take formless and void (repentant) humans and create His Kingdom.

The idea of Genesis 1 being a vital blueprint of redemption—including the Holy Spirit turbines on full power throughout the chapter—is validated in many ways through Scripture. In Genesis 1, the fluttering Holy Spirit combined with God's Words create new life and after each day God says, "It is good." In the New Testament, Paul writes, "But we all ... are being transformed into the same image from glory to glory, just as by the Spirit of the Lord" (2 Corinthians 3:18). Therefore, the "It is good" pronouncement each day represents a fresh glory. But note in both passages we are being changed by the Spirit of God and, as established in Genesis 1, the Spirit moves. It is His universal characteristic! The power plant of God's creative work requires the Holy Spirit to have freedom of movement—that's tongues.

Not a Conscious Connection

The pictures of the Holy Spirit in many biblical instances depict Him as one who functions more in our subconscious spirit than in our conscious awareness. A fluttering dove, blazing fire, pouring oil, blowing wind, and flowing water do not give the idea of one we can easily have a conversation with. In this regard, Paul spoke of the gift of prophecy being greater in a public service than tongues because when we pray in tongues, no one understands us. The Holy Spirit will invade our conscious mind and show us things "in part" through prophetic gifts, but when we yield to His turbine (tongues), He is doing His own business.

The Pattern

Genesis 1 combines God's fluttering Spirit with God's spoken words to form His creation. In the beginning of the Church age, God sends His Word (Jesus) and His fluttering Spirit into human bodies to commandeer their tongues and so execute His plan of redemption on their formless and void souls. I offer, therefore, according to the Genesis 1 pattern that the gift of tongues:

1. Divides light and darkness.
2. Executes the Word of God.
3. Creates new life ,systems.
4. Brings chaos into order.

I also maintain that the Holy Spirit turbine must continue to freely flow through regular devotional use of the gift of tongues throughout our lives, making it a vital aspect in God's master redemptive pattern. God has given us this gift to use at will. It is not a one-time experiential trophy. It is collaboration between God and His beloved. It requires a yielded servant, eyes to see, ears to hear, trust in God, and seasonal patience to see God's Kingdom come through this excellent gift. The rightly balanced use of the gift of tongues is destined to recreate lives, peoples, and cultures for God's glory.

Ask Yourself

* How do I presently discern between light and darkness in my life?
* Does the gift of tongues operate fully in my life?
* Am I willing to risk new spiritual things by faith?

*The rightly balanced
use of the gift of
tongues is destined
to recreate lives,
peoples, and cultures
for God's glory.*

Chapter Five

ON THE ROCK AND IN THE LIGHT

He is the Rock, His work is perfect; For all His ways are justice, A God of truth and without injustice; Righteous and upright is He.

Deuteronomy 32:4

I am the light of the world. He who follows Me shall not walk in darkness, but have the light of life.

John 8:12

SIGNPOST

About six or seven years into my walk with Jesus, I was praying in the Spirit one night and had a vision. As it began I was, in my mind's eye, in the midst of a vast dense jungle, seemingly endless thousands

57

of acres surrounding me with no way out. It was very dark but comfortable to my flesh, although I was essentially stuck there. I looked around and noticed that I stood in a small clearing and there was, shining through the jungle canopy above, a single beam of light coming down and illuminating a spot on the jungle floor. I then saw a large rock exactly under where the sunbeam fell and knew God wanted me on the rock and in the light (takes a real prophet to figure that one out!), so I climbed up on the rock. The word of the Lord spoken in my heart was, "No matter what, stay on the rock and in the light."

Soon it became uncomfortable. From the heat coming up from the rock to its hardness that hurt my body, the blazing sun on my head felt unbearable and the bright light hurt my eyes. But there was no relief and the word was unbending, "Stay on the rock and in the light." In the videotape of my vision, time passed and the discomfort increased. My skin began to crack, my face swelled, my eyes were burning. I became hotter and hotter as the cracks were weeping fluid from inside my body. Suddenly, as I looked out to the perimeter of the clearing, I could see the glowing eyes of nocturnal animals watching from the jungle and waiting. I was not sure if they were just curious or waiting to attack, but I knew they couldn't touch me as long as I was on the rock and in the light.

I stayed there a long, long time—too long. The heat increased and amplified and I just remained, God's word never wavering, "Stay on the rock and in the light." All of a sudden—POOF! The heat of my flesh reached flash point and instantly I was engulfed in flames. In sheer panic I began running around the clearing slapping at the fire, leaping and frantic. After only a few seconds I realized the fire didn't hurt in the least but the energy I felt from it was pure passion for God!

Now I was leaping and whirling and laughing and praising God. Still engulfed in flames, I saw that as I brushed against the undergrowth the fire lit the foliage and it began to burn and soon the entire jungle was on fire all around me. I was very much surprised that this jungle I thought was thousands of miles deep, was only about twenty yards wide and in an instant it burned down and I was standing in a wide open place.

I could see people gathered here and there and in my frenetic, on-fire state, I began running to different people and embracing them and then going to someone else and doing the same. And after I embraced each person they caught on fire too. Soon the fire spread to all the groups and all the people.

This vision has been a great source of strength, focus, and hope for me over the years. I can still feel the voice of God in me when things become seemingly unbearable, "Stay on the rock and in the light." Praying in tongues as a devotional practice thins the wall between Heaven and Earth so God's will can be revealed on a personal level.

> *Praying in tongues as a devotional practice thins the wall between Heaven and Earth so God's will can be revealed on a personal level.*

In the beginning God created the heavens and the earth. The earth was without form, and void; and darkness was on the face of the deep. And the Spirit of God was hovering over the face of the waters. Then God said, "Let there be light;" and there was light. And God saw the light, that it was good; and God divided the light from the darkness. God called the light Day, and the darkness He called Night. So the evening and the morning were the first day.

Genesis 1:1-5

We Must Pray in Tongues for the Holy Spirit to Move

As the first chapter of Scripture, Genesis 1 is the master pattern of redemption and as such, reveals universal truths. A vital observation from the second verse of the entire Bible, therefore, is that when God is present to create, the Holy Spirit moves—the Spirit is His point of entry with this dimension. Moving/hovering/fluttering across the face of the water shows that the Spirit is at work and in motion prepared to execute the Father's Word and so takes on the construction project. As soon as the Word comes, the Spirit moves to the fulfillment of the Word. Tongues are a portal of entry from His dimension into the world. Praying in tongues is yielding to the Spirit of God, so when God's Word comes, the Spirit works to build God's systems of life, wisdom, and productivity.

Praying in tongues is the Spirit praying in and through us. What the Spirit wants to birth or create in time and space has to be spoken in time and space. As the temple or the tabernacle of the Holy Spirit (1 Corinthians 3:16-17), each of us as a Christian incarnates Christ within us by His Spirit. We speak His words into our environment, thus bringing what God wills in Heaven to Earth. So God's creative activity of Genesis 1:2 (restated in John 1) continues through believers (the Church) in time and space today. As new creations in Christ by the Spirit, we pray in the Spirit with His tongue and speak Heaven into the Earth.

The Genesis 1 pattern reveals the sequence of events manifest in creation:

1. The Spirit moves over the face of the waters as darkness covers the deep (verse 2). That's the same thing Jesus did. Claiming Lordship over creation and boldly affirming the most controversial passage in the Scriptures, as darkness covered the deep Jesus moved (walked) across the face

of the waters, associating himself unashamedly with Genesis 1. We should be as courageous and unashamed in our recognition of Genesis 1 as truth.

What then does this say about the purpose of Genesis 1? There is but one pattern God uses to redeem formless and void things and this is it. As the Spirit of God turbine was integral in Genesis 1 and carried Jesus over the water, the Holy Spirit now moves inside God's people (using tongues) to marry Heaven and Earth thereby accomplishing redemption.

This is an aside but it should be mentioned. My wrestling match to be at peace with Genesis 1 as truth in the face of science was resolved through Christ. Our faith rests in Jesus, who is the creative Word of God. He is the "beginning" of our faith and all truth is assessed through Him. Our eggs are in His basket. The miracle of Cana at Galilee, turning water to wine, is an example of God making something instantly that has all the properties of something old. The wine Jesus instantly made from water would bear all of the scientific markings of a sophisticated product requiring natural processes, human effort and ... time. In the same way the universe and all in it are constructed as a vintage wine; perfectly aged.

The reported "best wine" served at this wedding must have certainly seemed to be perfectly aged and the skilled steward might have even discerned the region where the grapes were grown and the vintage year—no way it was two minutes old—that would be impossible! Creation is the same way. The universe seems billions of years old and fossils and carbon dating have sent the Church into a tizzy. But Jesus leaves us a key of understanding. The Spirit draws from God's timeless dimension and natural processes either occur in timelessness and are instantly brought here or are simply created complete with the appearance of process. It was true with the wine and it is true with creation. Time is a non-issue in God's Spirit.

2. **God said, "Let there be light."** The Holy Spirit turbine executes God's Word introducing light to the darkness of human depravity. There is no genuine illumination without God's Word and the moving Holy Spirit.

3. **God saw the light was** *good.* Light shining in the darkness causes God pleasure and then the Holy Spirit transports the Father's pleasure to the human soul. This is where emotion comes in. *"...the joy of the LORD is your strength"* (Nehemiah 8:10). *"In Your presence is fullness of joy; At Your right hand are pleasures forevermore"* (Psalms 16:11).

4. **God divided the light from the darkness.** This is a great key to understanding the purpose of using

tongues as a devotional prayer language. Praying in tongues separates the light from the darkness and on this point we will elaborate.

Dividing the Light from the Darkness

"...and God divided the light from the darkness" (Genesis 1:4). The first job of the fluttering Spirit of God is dividing light from darkness. This is an interesting thought as it speaks to the issues and agendas of the human heart. It seems today that many want, on one hand, to oversimplify complex truth or, on the other, consider truth too nuanced for anyone to be truly committed to unchanging values.

The modern world has adopted moral relativism and thrown out God's commandments to answer what they consider to be the ever-changing, too complex standards of truth. It seems like our light and darkness are too intermingled to clearly identify consistent standards of truth. We also see many Christians and religious zealots oversimplify all truth and jam every issue into predetermined categories rendering wisdom as elementary school-level rules of do's and don'ts.

Think of mixing together white laundry with colored. This is not done out of concern that the colored clothes might be ruined, but the white—the colored dyes dull the white. That's why praying in the Spirit separates the light from the darkness. The white laundry separated is God's Word in our minds becoming electrified by God's turbine (Holy Ghost tongues), which makes them exceedingly white and the stark contrast to the darkness of sin and selfishness becomes unmistakable.

Next, the electrified Scriptures connect with other electrified Scriptures, creating in the mind networks of understanding and ultimately producing the principle thing: wisdom. And wisdom is the complete wardrobe of white and answers the hardest of all questions, "How then shall we live?" That is why Jesus, whom the Spirit came to replace, said, *"You are already clean because of the word which I have spoken to you"* (John 15:3). The Word and the Spirit bring brilliant light and life.

I recently listened to a message online from a well-known contemporary pastor. He was speaking about the Sermon on the Mount and explaining to his church that unless one understands the cultural context of Jesus' day and the social issues in vogue during those times it is impossible to really understand His intended teaching on the issue of divorce. He essentially said that we now have better understanding and have outgrown this Scripture. Unbelievable!

Although understanding history and culture can be enriching to our faith, the problem with a teaching like this is that it implies that studying the Word of God is not sufficient and one must possess graduate degree levels of historical knowledge to truly understand Jesus. This is classic religious smoke and mirrors because it takes the ability to understand the Word of God away from the hungry saint and puts the interpretation of the Scripture in the hands of an elite academic class of leaders.

Jesus picked His disciples for a reason. His leaders were not known to be formally well educated but were all gainfully employed (that's an interesting concept). When finally they became the leaders of the Church, they did not teach the new believers to look for loopholes in Jesus' teaching. They instead reinforced everything He said by creating continuity with the Old Covenant at times and contrast with the Old Covenant at other times. At all times they sought to implement the Master's words to the fullest. The Church's job is to submit to the Master's teaching, not plot convoluted user-friendly theology.

Trying to justify sinful modern culture by playing bait and switch with Jesus' words looks desperate and reveals a lack of the Holy Spirit's presence in the modern Church. One who invests enough time with a submissive heart praying in the Spirit divides God's Word with amazing clarity. This one is able to discern light from darkness and recognizes Jesus' Words as trans-cultural and germane to all people for all times. As Jesus said: *"Heaven and earth will pass away, but My words will by no means pass away"* (Luke 21:33). It is Jesus' words that will judge all humanity. His true disciples will always be repulsed by sin, not looking for a special license to continue in it.

> *One who invests enough time with a submissive heart praying in the Spirit divides Gods' Word with amazing clarity.*

The greatest victory for the Spirit-filled believer is discovering Jesus' intended meaning, and proving His words as the most perfect and concentrated capsules of truth in the universe. The Master's words are immutable, unchangeable, trans-cultural truth, which every nation, people, and tribe will ultimately bow to and be judged by. Separating light from darkness by the Holy Spirit, growing in understanding and implementing strategies born of the produced wisdom is the only mission of the saint of God and the Church of Jesus Christ.

The fluttering Spirit of God (tongues) divides the light from the darkness both in Genesis 1 and in the lives of believers praying in the Spirit. The great personal benefit of praying in tongues is allowing God to divide your own light and darkness, seeing sin (especially your own) as exceedingly sinful and Christ's righteousness as exceedingly brilliant. A famous restaurant chain has a meat-lover's pizza. Praying in tongues will produce a righteousness-lover's life!

When we first receive Jesus as Lord and Savior, our soul has been invaded with light. However, the light of Jesus' truth is intermingled with the darkness of a world filled with old beliefs, customs, and practices. Our light and darkness are all blended together in our contemporary, relativistic culture, which has no absolute truth. Consequently, people, as sheep without shepherds, will typically be open for deception and follow any voice that makes sense to them. This was the problem with the Church at Laodicea in Revelation 3 as we'll see in our next chapter.

Ask Yourself

* Is Scripture bright, clear, and sharp for you, or is it dull, muddled, and fuzzy?

* Do you really understand the truth of God's Word as you pray or do you remain confused?

* When you pray without tongues, do you feel energized, empowered, enlightened, and enabled, or do you quickly tire of prayer and move on to other things?

* Have you seen the invisible when you pray and been electrified by the miraculous, or do you simply languish in the common and ordinary stuff of existence?

* Is your prayer life creative or just repetitious?

Chapter Six

THANK YOU

His lord said to him, "Well done, good and faithful servant; you were faithful over a few things, I will make you ruler over many things. Enter into the joy of your lord."

Matthew 25:21

SIGNPOST

Our original church facility in Margaretville, NY, received much renovation and expansion in the first few years of our ministry. Eventually it became obvious that if we were going to fulfill God's vision for Catskill Mountain Christian Center, we would need an expanded location. The perfect spot opened up in 1998 when the Great American supermarket on

69

Main Street went out of business. I immediately felt this was the ideal space God had for us. Although priced way out of our range, I received an amazing creative financing strategy in prayer one night and pitched it to the supermarket's corporate owner. The plan included very little money down and a graduated payment plan for three years with a balloon payment for the balance at the end of this time.

It took a long time haggling with banks, lawyers, and the owners, but in the end the deal was sealed exactly to the penny of the plan God gave me and we owned the building. Next we hired John Maxwell's affiliate organization, Injoy Stewardship Services, to conduct a capital stewardship campaign to raise money for the renovation build-out. We did as much of the construction work as possible ourselves to keep costs down. By Christmas 2000, we had our first service in our new Main Street location. The renovated supermarket on almost two acres was a painted cinderblock structure and not much to look at from the outside, but inside was all brand new with a 300-seat sanctuary plus very pleasant and adequate office and program space.

Full of excitement, we went to work with a vengeance, holding spiritual and social events just waiting for the growth to come. We started a weekly free-of-charge senior citizen's dinner club, hosted Christian concerts, brought in various evangelists along with operating our full-time Christian Academy and all the other whistles and bells of a modern, living church. We worked hard, prayed hard, and played hard.

We always conduct our ministry as a full-time endeavor. If we own the building 24/7, we do our best to fill every square inch of it as much as possible with life-giving, Kingdom-building activities. And so we worked and prayed and prayed and worked and waited for growth—nothing. In fact, we lost a few key families in the building process and transition. Our new location was not attracting anyone fresh like we'd hoped. One, two, three years passed and we picked up very few new families. This new facility was a lot more expensive to operate, so money became really tight.

Then a series of difficult things began to happen that affected me personally. From family issues to health issues to church problems and lean financial times, things became significantly harder and less fulfilling. The apostolic network we were a faithful part of from the beginning of our ministry unraveled, crashed, and burned in a most painful death. This left us an independent church without any official

*affiliation, which is absolutely against my nature—
I really love connectedness. During this strenuous
time another misunderstanding took place between
me, another church, and my elders that put me back
on my heels and left me walking ugly.*

*Then one cold Sunday morning in January as I sat
in the front row, and our worship leader Gina Barto
and her daughters were singing special music during
the offering, I had a moment of clarity. My bruised
heart was flooded with fulfillment as I saw this lovely
local family singing praises to Jesus and testifying of
His love in a living church in this nicely appointed
modern sanctuary. I said within myself to the Lord,
"Thank you, Jesus. Now I understand. Now I can
see that all of the effort, the blood, sweat, and tears
were worth it to have this beautiful place and see the
faith of this dear family validated as they sing of your
love here smack in the middle of our community."*

*Instantly the voice of God responded to me. I'm
assuming it was an angel, but it might very well have
been Jesus himself. Although it was not a physical
voice, I could tell it came from
in front of me and to my left
side slightly. The space from
which the voice projected could
not have been more than a*

**God spoke only
two words to me,
"Thank you."**

foot away. I could feel where the voice was coming from. The speech was kingly or regal and filled with density, love, dignity, and respect. It was intentional, measured, and very distinct. There was no mistaking it. Only two words, "Thank you."

It is important to say that receiving gratitude from God for doing the work He's called me to do was not in my theology. I never expected Him to say it and His graciousness instantly overwhelmed me. I'm not a big crier, especially as far as preacher-types go, but my heart just gushed as the healing of these words swept through my soul. I always tell people I'm a pretty cheap date for God because it just took two words to heal, reignite, and recalibrate my trajectory in Him. It was awesome!

With all the voices from inside and outside the church offering teachings, opinions, criticism, hostility, rebuke, and citing modern trends, it is sometimes hard to know, even in your own heart, if you're doing the right thing. Researchers are publishing harrowing statistics about the state of the Church in America and in this world of mega-churches and TV preachers pulling people in every which way and offering grace discounts at bargain basement prices, remaining true to Jesus' specific vision is only possible, in my humble opinion, through much prayer in the Spirit.

Not too many people think very highly of a small rural church in the mountains of upstate New York. The point of saying this is that these two simple words from God cut through the cloud of subterfuge and let me know that I had indeed been on the course He set for me. I remember saying to myself in my heart, "I always thought I was doing this by God's Holy Spirit and right faith." The confirmation I felt from the divine pat-on-the-back was palpable!

Now as an offspring of Father Abraham, I also tend to be always looking to gain advantage when dealing with God. I love the account in Genesis chapter 15 when God speaks to Abram and says essentially, "I am your reward." Instantly Abram retorts by asking, "Then what will you give me?" So in thinking about the two words God had spoken to me it became obvious that a great King would never intentionally express His appreciation to one of His loyal subjects for their faithful work without giving gifts! Woo-hoo! I knew something good must be on the way.

Like the certain turning of seasons, from that point forward everything changed. Starting within days of that event, over the next twelve months my personal life and our church were exponentially blessed. Three different men came from three different sets of unrelated circumstances and through them I received healing in my body, book writing opportunities, a model for a wonderful food outreach ministry, a major earning opportunity for the church, and by year's end I was holding the gift of a half-million dollar check to help construct a beautiful, state-of-the-art worship chapel on our Main Street property. Like the magi bearing gifts to help Mary and Joseph fund the baby Jesus' upbringing, these wise men showed up, practically out of nowhere, bringing gifts to support Jesus' work in our town and then they each returned from whence they came.

Praying in tongues sets up the supernatural component of Christian life bringing God's will in Heaven to Earth.

When Praying in Tongues, the Spirit is Moving

According to Genesis 1, in the beginning the Earth was without form and void. Form relates to organized structure and void means it was empty. This shows that God will only build on a place with no existing structures or knowledge. He is willing to renovate neither an existing universe nor one's personal belief system. God's work, starting with the foundation, must be new from the ground up—all or nothing. That's why Jesus called it being "born again."

So even before the foundations were laid, the presence of the Holy Spirit was already moving over "the face of the waters" in the darkness. As the Psalm says, *"Where can I go from Your Spirit? Or where can I flee from Your presence? ...The darkness and the light are both alike to You"* (Psalm 139:7;12). Now when we pray in tongues the Holy Spirit moves over "the deep" which is the entire unseen realm.

The *deep* speaks to the unknown depths of our own souls but also includes the spiritual realm in general. The *deep* is the unseen world and is prophetically represented in Genesis 1 by the deep of a sea. That's why when Jesus walked on the sea he was, in fact, walking in Genesis 1. Jesus was in the Spirit, moving across the face of the waters. The gospel in one version says He would have passed them by. He was simply in the Spirit being carried wherever the Spirit led (see Romans 8).

When praying in tongues, the mind is uninformed as the Spirit moves across the deep. The one praying goes along for the ride and may or may not be let in on the purpose. Tongues are subconscious—your spirit is speaking. This is of eternal substance and in union with the Holy Spirit as He uses your speaking ability to vocalize His own language and do His own business. You are not invited into that knowledge the way Adam was not invited into the knowledge of the forbidden tree.

That is not to say that your mind has nothing to do while you pray in tongues. Your mind's job is to worship, praise, and intercede as well as ponder/inquire and stretch in the light of the Scriptures and the issues of your life. Most people are quick to tell me how they pray in tongues while driving the car, sort of double-dipping, which I also do. However, that does not allow the full probing concentration and mental engagement of dedicated prayer-in-the-Spirit time. Praying in the Spirit is a learned discipline.

The mind must learn to become active in God while praying in the Spirit. Keeping the mind engaged is a major problem even when praying with your intellect, which is why Jesus criticized the Pharisees for making long prayers with their hearts far away. One can pray and have all kinds of agendas other than a pure heart before the Lord in prayer. Some people show off or feign humility while praying publicly and others even in private say the words of prayers with a distracted mind. I've learned from my wife that talking to her with my mind somewhere else is not appreciated. How much more God?

The mind must learn to become active in God while praying in the Spirit.

In order for redemption to occur, systems of belief and competing ideologies must be yielded. The heart must be humble and teachable before God will build anything. Praying in tongues causes the Spirit to bring these unacceptable competing issues into the light. They must be jettisoned because a full heart of self-will has no room for God's new creation. Repentance from the conviction of the Holy Ghost must precede new light and construction. Any hybrid is unacceptable.

When we pray in tongues, the Holy Spirit is active within our bodies to identify and level existing mental attitudes, opposing knowledge, memories, commitments, or allegiances that, if not yielded, will prevent the inner Kingdom revolution. Building God's new creation on existing values is like renovating a tarpaper shanty by landscaping, adding an in-ground pool, and putting golden fixtures in the bathroom. It produces a Frankenstein's monster type of dysfunctional Christian.

Praying in tongues with the heart open to God's Word will receive flashes of prophetic reality and build a well-balanced acceptable life of great value to the Lord and His business. Life will develop in season without having to spawn numerous Ishmaels along the way.

Tongues Separates Light From Darkness

We made the point in the previous chapter that exercising the gift of tongues divides the light from the darkness. This is seen in Genesis 1:2-4 as Scripture identifies the fluttering Spirit of God present from the very beginning. It is our main point that the fluttering is prophetic of tongues.

This fluttering Spirit of God is now active through tongues. This demonstrates a universal principle: God's words are electrified and executed in the material world by the moving of the Spirit. The first two things God commands in Genesis are the introduction of light, and the separating of light from darkness. Therefore, to the one who has received light (salvation) into his darkness, a main ongoing activity of the Spirit is dividing the two by praying in tongues with an open heart. Darkness (sin) is identified and God's words come alive as the

God's words are electrified and executed in the material world by the moving of the Spirit.

Spirit electrifies them. The contrast becomes clear for the one who prays in tongues.

Ask Yourself

* Are you hungry for depth in your prayer life? Then pray in the Spirit. Deep calls unto deep!
* Do you desire to see God's will in Heaven become a reality in your life? Then pray in tongues!
* Tired of the ordinary and commonplace? Are you tired enough to begin praying in tongues?

*Praying in tongues
sets up the
supernatural
component of
Christian life
bringing God's will
in Heaven to Earth.*

Chapter Seven

A WALL OF DARKNESS MOVES

For we do not wrestle against flesh and blood, but against principalities, against powers, against the rulers of the darkness of this age, against spiritual hosts of wickedness in the heavenly places.

Ephesians 6:12

SIGNPOST

During the first year and a half after I was filled with the Holy Spirit and praying in tongues for at least an hour a day, we tried a number of different churches but could not find one that we could connect with. Finally, one day we visited Ravena

Bible Training Center near Albany, NY, led by Pastor Alan Babcock. Within five minutes we knew this would be home. I still remember our first time there. A tall redheaded man with a great red beard met us at the back door and began talking to me like I was his old friend. He introduced himself as Jim and proceeded to tell about how much he loved Jesus! No icebreaker asking me if I liked to hunt or fish like you get from most Christian guys. I guess he just assumed if I was in church I must be interested in God. He was right and over the next few years Jim Bunyar and I became very close friends. We spoke many hours about Jesus.

My overall experience during the first years in the church was nothing short of idyllic. Pastor Alan was wise and warm and intelligent. He was Spirit-filled and prayed in tongues—a lot! We came to meet weekly so he could teach and disciple me. We talked for hours as I downloaded all I could get my mind around. There were times it seemed there was a haze in his small office—the glory cloud of God was so close through our holy discussions of God's Word that it became visible. The first few years in Ravena were such a wonderful season that I caught hold of a burning passionate love for the church.

One Sunday morning a guest minister came to preach.

He was introduced as Pastor Alan's original pastor from out of state, and he was going to speak this morning on a very important topic. The topic turned out to be abortion and, although I was principally pro-life, the picture he painted revealed the sober underlying truth that every abortion kills an innocent baby. He said it was not enough to be against abortion, but churches must provide an alternative. The church must be willing to not only explain the ugly truth to the pregnant mothers, but also support them through their pregnancies and walk with them through decisions of adoption or raising their babies. He had founded a pregnancy distress center that was doing this kind of work very successfully and saving babies' lives.

As the minister shared statistics and details of the processes by which abortions take place, both Nancy's and my hearts were pounding at the silent atrocity happening to unborn babies all around us. I guess we were somewhat naïve to the cultural reality that had taken us so far so fast from the God-fearing, America-the-good caricature I still held in my heart. On the drive home from church we both confirmed what the other was feeling—we need to be involved in this work. As soon as we arrived home, I called Pastor Alan and signed us up, volunteering to lead or do whatever necessary to combat this evil.

The first thing organized was a steering committee to determine the vision and mission of this ministry. Because it was a women-oriented outreach, Nancy became the organizational leader under Pastor Alan. We had little children at the time and I was working day shifts, so I stayed home with the kids when Nancy went to the evening meetings. The nice thing about young children (six years old and below) is they are all in bed by eight o'clock. This left time for me to intercede in the Spirit for the steering committee meeting and to pray against this darkness in our land called abortion.

A wonderful aspect of prayer is effort. The Bible says that Jesus prayed so hard He was sweating blood! "And being in agony, He prayed more earnestly. Then His sweat became like great drops of blood falling down to the ground" (Luke 22:44). In the Book of James, Scripture makes it clear that our natural abilities are no different than Elijah's and he prayed so hard that it stopped raining. He prayed again and the rain returned. "Elijah was a man with a nature like ours, and he prayed earnestly that it would not rain; and it did not rain on the land for three years and six months. And he prayed again, and the heaven gave rain, and the earth produced its fruit" (James 5:17-18).

That night with our children tucked safely in bed and Nancy in Ravena working out the future of what we hoped would be a ministry to save babies and lead people to Jesus, I prayed. I prayed hard. I prayed long. I prayed in the Spirit. As always I began with praise, worship, and thanksgiving, but then, in my own words I came against the darkness and every evil associated with abortion in Jesus' name. I pushed and pushed with my faith against this wall of darkness. I was incensed at the rudeness of the devil lying to women claiming that what is growing inside is not a baby. I felt the righteous anger of the Lord and could sense the attention of the spiritual world. Suddenly, something happened.

As I pushed, I distinctly felt the great wall of darkness giving way! Not too far but far enough that I felt it. As I prayed in tongues, the wall of evil resistance certainly didn't fall down, just moved significantly backward. The joy that filled my soul was nothing less than extreme! I leapt

As I prayed in tongues, the wall of evil resistance certainly didn't fall down, just moved significantly backward.

and praised the Lord because I sensed intrinsically that the prayer had moved the darkness out of the way for the establishment of the pro-life ministry.

That would not be the end of the prayers on behalf of this work, but that was the moment when the momentum changed.

The rest of the story just sounds like a well-executed plan coming together. Within the year every necessary door opened and Abow Pregnancy Distress Center became a reality. A perfect location opened up which was owned by a Catholic man who shared our concern for the unborn and he gave us the office space at a fraction of the normal rental fee. We trained volunteer staff and under Pastor Babcock's leadership, Nancy and her friend Andrea led the center saving lives every year and sharing the gospel with hundreds of women. We left for Margaretville five years later and Abow was still thriving and shining the light of God's love for mothers and their babies.

The Bible says, "The effective, fervent prayer of a righteous man avails much" (James 5:16).

Laodicea—Light and Darkness Intermingled

And to the angel of the church of the Laodiceans write, "These things says the Amen, the Faithful and True Witness, the Beginning of the creation of God: I know your works, that you are neither cold nor hot. I could wish you were cold or hot. So then, because you are lukewarm, and neither cold nor hot, I will spit you out of My mouth. Because you say, 'I am rich, have become wealthy, and have need of nothing'—and do not know that you are wretched, miserable, poor, blind, and naked—I counsel you to buy from Me gold refined in the fire, that you may be rich; and white garments, that you may be clothed, that the shame of your nakedness may not be revealed; and anoint your eyes with eye salve, that you may see. As many as I love, I rebuke and chasten. Therefore be zealous and repent. Behold, I stand at the door and knock. If anyone hears My voice and opens the door, I will come in to him and dine with him, and he with Me. To him who overcomes I will grant to sit with Me on My throne, as I also overcame and sat down with My Father on His throne. He who has an ear, let him hear what the Spirit says to the churches."

Revelation 3:14-22

The Laodiceans were lukewarm believers. They believed the success gained as they increased in wealth and physical security after being saved proved that they were now whole, but they didn't know their dirty, impoverished mind-life seriously needed some cleansing. "Because you say, 'I am rich, have become wealthy, and have need of nothing'—and <u>do not know</u> that you are wretched, miserable, poor, blind, and naked" (underlining added). Notice the phrase, "Do not know." Their focus in the gospel was on physical prosperity, which can be seen, and not on the more important unseen issue of a clean, forgiving, worshipful, and loving heart. In their minds and hearts, light and darkness were all confused like a tangled ball of string. They thought that their wealth and security were the object of the Kingdom and were blind to their own evil hearts and impoverished souls.

Praying in Tongues Separates Light and Darkness

Without praying in tongues with the light of the Word of God, it is hard to maintain focus on the benefits that can't be seen. The Spirit's work is within the soul (the deep) separating the light of God's Word and the darkness of sin and the demonic realm. Our work is to maintain submission to the authority and Spirit of

Praying in tongues provides true illumination that can only come from God.

His Word and stretch so the illumination can come. Praying in tongues provides the true illumination that can only come from God.

The Laodiceans had the light of faith in Jesus, but their light and darkness were mixed and confused; they were not aware of how sick their souls were. Without humble hearts and the dividing Spirit there was no inner horror standing between Jesus' brilliant white words and their unclean disobedient minds. This is a huge mistake and the rebuke from the Lord is scathing!

For this misdirected kind of Christian for whom wealth is the main objective of their walk and the only measuring stick of righteousness, there is no peace. The

Genesis 1 pattern of redemption shows us that God builds very specific pre-planned items and systems on certain days and in our lives. If God desires to work inside under the hood on a day when we will only welcome His work that leads to wealth and security, we can end up praying against the very thing He's trying to do. Scripture teaches how loving money can lead us into evil. If the heart is humble and open before God when praying in tongues, God will set the agenda and build based on His timing and wisdom.

As we ask, seek, and knock, Jesus reveals truth about our situations and ourselves. Praying in tongues clears the clouded perspective we have of ourselves and what's happening around us. Often when I find myself driving in rain or snow, my car's windshield clouds over and I must turn on the defroster in order for the windshield to clear and give me the vision I need to see where I'm going. When I pray in tongues, the eyes of my spirit clear so I can see where God is leading me.

That is not to say we shouldn't pray for what we want and need. We should enthusiastically pray for every good thing we need and want. Prayer is collaboration and if you will pray in the Spirit allowing God to access your vocal chords for His purpose He will give you the desires of your heart. Interestingly, the word *desire* is "de" which means "from" and "sire" which is "father." As we pray, therefore, the Father's desires and our desires merge satisfying both in the deepest possible way. Prayer is not earning righteousness. We are not paid for the time we labor in prayer. Rather, we grow in relationship with God so that we develop intimacy with Him. Your responsibility is to pray in the Spirit giving your vocal cords to His purposes, His desires.

When we pray in tongues we are speaking angelic language (1 Corinthians 13:1). The angels have tasks to do, and the Holy Spirit dispatches them in their own language. If I go to China they speak Chinese. If I go to Kenya they speak Kiswahili. If I go to the Spirit they speak angel. Because God has invited His children to participate with angels by speaking their language, it MUST be important business!

When we pray in tongues we are speaking angelic language.

As a baby Christian I loved the faith, healing, and prosperity messages because I needed them. Still do. Also, the faith message has a very resonant ring of truth when you refuse to turn your eyes from Jesus' words to "say unto this mountain be removed and cast into the sea… when you pray believe you've received it and you'll have it." I think the prosperity message haters do not have much empathy toward the poor and broken, and I have never heard a plausible explanation for these and many other Scriptures from anyone but the faith-camp brethren.

In those early days after working all day and spending family time, I would pray in tongues an hour or two each evening, study my Bible and watch many of the preachers on TBN. What I learned through this boot camp season is that praying in tongues and confessing all of

God's blessings along with working hard and carrying the normal burdens of life while keeping God's Word in my face, among other things, brought a whole lot of sin in me to the surface. The Laodiceans were apparently missing something!

As I did this though, and stayed the course, I fell more and more in love with Jesus and at the same time saw more and more junk in me. Junk is a nice way of saying sin. Praying in tongues while on a diet of God's Word makes one painfully aware and uncomfortable about personal sin. It is the Spirit and the Word that bring life!

Praying in Tongues Makes you Want to try Works of Faith

I remember trying to figure out how the faith/confession component worked while driving in our junk-bucket of an old car down to the new car dealer in Catskill. I was only saved for about a year, but I really needed a car big enough for our growing family. I was learning the Word and praying hours each day, so I decided to apply my newly acquired faith lessons focusing on a new car and boldly claim it in Jesus' name. I drove around the lot with Nancy and the kids in the car and found the biggest, shiniest, fanciest African Queen-like of a three-seater station wagon (before minivans were invented) complete with wood grain sides, a roof-rack, and electric windows!

I got out of our car, walked over and laid my hands

on the hood of the African Queen-wagon and began to confess at the top of my lungs that this was my car and thank you Jesus for giving it to me. I had my eyes tightly shut most of the time due to the overwhelming embarrassment and Nan and the kids were slunk down in their seats hiding as I prayed on. The salesman coming out to greet me did a hot-foot about-face when he heard me crying out, and I have never felt more unspiritual in my life. My face red, my heart pounding, and not feeling at all like a faith man, I finished and went home. (By the way, I do not in the slightest regret doing this. I was trying to work it out.)

I never did get that car but my story does illustrate an important point. Praying in tongues makes you confident that you are approaching God's dimension and sometimes it takes awkward steps of faith to find your footing. Christianity might be defined as the business of working out your faith. It is not an exact science any more than a baby learning to walk is, and each of us approaches God with unique issues, needs, and wants.

Sometimes it takes awkward steps of faith before you find your footing.

God is never offended that you ask and keep on asking. God rewards persistence. The Laodicean problem was that in focusing on becoming prosperous and finally receiving it, they neglected the rest of the Bible calling them to personal holiness, sacrifice, and love. I once had a thought that someday on a ministry trip to the backside of someplace, I'm going to end up doing itinerate ministry in a vaguely familiar looking station wagon made in the early eighties.

Why was the Lord's rebuke against Laodicea so scathing? *"...spit you out of my mouth."* You can feel the heat coming from the Master after these people were given so much by Him. It is because they obtained prosperity but the beguiling aspect of worldly wealth sidetracked them and they did not stay in both the Spirit and the Word. They thought the prosperity was the destination when in fact their souls were better off when they were poor. They became satisfied. The flow of Kingdom funding dammed up in their bank accounts like the Dead Sea.

We pray in tongues because the Holy Spirit must move, and we must move with Him. Wealth is not a destination, it is a pool to flow into and out of—a war chest for Kingdom-building. Praying in tongues keeps spiritual vision open for God to direct the war chest distribution through his stewards. God desires for His Kingdom work to be collaboration between His Spirit, His children, and His angels. He deposits money in our banks and gives us ideas for prospering in business to fund His work. He is the God of infinite creativity and works with partners to manage construction.

The Laodiceans took care of their own children and future with their money and felt righteous for it. But it was really only put in their hands to steward it for His business and they instead became a dead pool. They were increased with wealth and then lost their Kingdom vision.

Look how mad this made Jesus. He said I am going to "...*spit you out of my mouth.*" Literally spitting mad! How can a Christian be satisfied when:

* So many are going to hell?
* So many are starving?
* So many are poor?
* The Church has become more like a McDonalds play area than a nation with a great and noble purpose?
* When so many preach feel-good messages to people whose souls are wretched, poor, miserable, blind, and naked?

Candy-throwing, shallow preachers are lying to blind, wretched people. Their half-truths and superficial clichés are filling a Nazi death train to hell. Christ warned, *"Because you say, 'I am rich, have become wealthy, and have need of nothing and do not know....'"*

When you pray in tongues, He moves over your deep soul. He bothers you. He upsets you. He impassions you.

> *Praying in tongues deepens you so the shallow trappings of the world do not satisfy.*

You are stricken with both Jesus' passion and His compassion. Entrusted wealth is not to cause His people to be satisfied but is meant to flow through them. The faithful steward will always be entrusted by the Master to fully accomplish the Master's objectives and there is always enough to care well for the steward. Praying in tongues deepens you so the shallow trappings of the world do not satisfy.

Questions are Answered

The Laodicean dilemma also illuminates two of the great questions of all times:

* What is the expected benefit of the gospel in this life; and
* How can one discern God's pleasure from His anger?

We read Scriptures that make us feel good and skip over ones that don't. We listen to preachers who we agree with and find a church that's comfortable. If we're rebellious, we ignore church altogether and find obscure verses releasing us from accountability to covering. If we profit on an investment, it was the Lord, but if we lose our shirts because of a stupid decision, it was the devil. We use God as a household idol and rub His belly to get good fortune but do not internalize the hard sayings of the Word—and there are plenty. All of these are indicators of Laodicean lukewarm religion or, for our purpose, intermingled light and darkness.

The Laodiceans were not unbelievers. They were brethren, but they were so far gone that Jesus says to them, *"You do not know that you are wretched, miserable, poor, blind, and naked."* Those are terrible things to be called.

Exercising the gift
of tongues divides
the light from
the darkness.

Ask Yourself

*   Are you praying for what you
    want or what God wants?
*   Are you seeking Him or just stuff from Him?
*   Are you willing to humble yourself
    and refuse to take pride in what
    you have or have done?
*   Will you pray in tongues to separate
    light from darkness in your life?

EMPOWERING ANGELS

"Though I speak with the tongues of men and of angels..."

1 Corinthians 13:1

SIGNPOST

Praying in tongues empowers angels. It is their language. Praying in tongues clears the road ahead so that grace is available to deliver you through troubles. Praying in tongues lays groundwork for God's Kingdom to come. Praying in tongues is a grace generator.

Approaching the New Year of 2009, I sought the Lord for the coming year. I felt moved to reorder my personal prayer time to begin spending the lunch hour Monday through Friday praying in our church sanctuary. Honestly, this was not a sacrifice because praying in the Holy Spirit is something I really love to do. I also know that praying in a particular physical place and investing time in a location changes the ruling spiritual balance.

I maintained that regimen of prayer from January 2009 all the way into 2011. The prayer surely bore benefits as I could see an increase in God moving, protecting us, and providing for us. During January of each of year, I opened this prayer hour up to members of our church so everyone could get their year kicked off right. But I particularly like to pray in solitude, like Jesus who often went alone into the wilderness to pray. Adding even one person to private prayer time changes the dynamic. True intimacy is really only between two—you and the Lord.

I have learned it takes spiritual eyes to see God in events and circumstances. Jesus said the pure in heart will see God, so seeing God at work in circumstances requires praying in the Spirit, dividing light from darkness. Praying in tongues

Seeing God at work in circumstances requires praying in the Spirit, dividing light from darkness.

prepares the future so when opportunity comes or crisis hits, the angels have gone before you to prepare the way. In that moment, if you have spiritually paved the way, you'll see God as clearly as you can see the sunrise. In August 2011, having prayed my hour in the sanctuary each day for two years and eight months, a miracle happened that actually began as a tragedy.

On Sunday morning, August 28, 2011, I showed up at the church at 6:30 a.m. to prepare for service. By 9:30 a.m., I was evacuated as our rural region was making the national news. Tropical Storm Irene had made her way 150 miles inland and devastated our entire region with terrible flooding. Our little village of Margaretville and the greater region were ravaged by this disaster with hundreds of homes, businesses, and roads either badly damaged or completely destroyed. Our town was left looking like a bombed-out city from WWII Europe.

A disaster of this magnitude makes everyone feel sick with almost a dizzying disorientation. Peoples' homes and livelihoods were gone. Bridges and roads were out. The only real supermarket in the area was gutted and the main drug store had been leveled. Our church's 7,200 square foot program building was flooded with water, wiping out all flooring along with some other losses, but we were very fortunate compared to those who lost everything. Jesus said the rain falls on the just and the unjust, so when disaster strikes Christians should never be surprised when we share the sufferings of our neighbors.

What happened next was a miracle. God's grace was evident right from the start. Like Jesus distributing the loaves and fishes through the disciples' hands, our Catskill Mountain Christian Center family members started reporting for Kingdom duty the very next morning and the Lord began multiplying resources. In short, I have never seen anything like it!

It is obvious to the perceptive when something takes on a life of its own and when an investment is returning more than it should. Over the next month through our modestly sized rural ministry, incredible things happened.

First, all of the carpeting in our program building had to be torn out and the facility outfitted as a disaster relief headquarters. Next, a veritable army of church members and volunteers from out of town reported for duty as our church leaders each took areas of oversight and organized the effort. It ran like a finely tuned machine with amazing unity and productivity.

Over the next days we put up mess hall tents on the church lawn and converted our food assistance program to an emergency food relief operation. Our work crews restored nearly a hundred homes and businesses to habitable conditions by mucking basements, removing appliances, tearing out carpets, and whatever else was needed to restore living conditions (this was dirty, smelly, and backbreaking work). These crews consisted of many church members and over 200 volunteers from out of town who came from far and wide to lend a hand.

We worked with regional and national agencies including churches, village, town, state, and federal agencies, the American Red Cross, the National Guard, and others. We supplied the food, cooked and served over 4,000 hot, fresh meals for victims and workers. Our own team of church leaders and members logged upwards of 5,000 hours and our ministry gave out $100,000 in groceries and household supplies to over 500 affected families. We provided money to many in need.

Besides the hard numbers, the spirit of our relief effort cannot be denied. There was such amazing unity and good will that everyone noticed. The thing is, it all felt completely natural and organic—as if it had its own life. Emotionally distraught victims, business owners, and community leaders came and poured their hearts out, many breaking down in tears at the loss of their homes and so much of *their precious community. Through all of this our church family smiled, worked tirelessly, comforted neighbors, fed people, and ministered. We prayed for scores of people and shared Jesus' love in an open door like I've never seen in my life.*

I believe with all of my heart that praying in tongues an hour a day for two years and eight months prior to the flood prepared the spiritual environment for this success. I am not taking anything away from the heroic efforts of so many of those who worked so hard, but I am saying that when we release the Holy Spirit by praying in tongues the angels prepare the future. In a time when a thousand things could go wrong, very intricate coordination is required and most people's emotions are raw. Finding ourselves in an envelope of God's grace is unmistakably wondrous and awesome.

What you pray through tongues into the atmosphere shapes the future. Ever walk into

What you pray through tongues into the atmosphere shapes the future.

a non-descript room with an interior decorator? HGTV has all types of programs that show how remodeling and paint can transform a worthless, drab space into a stunning, usable room. The Holy Spirit uses the paint and the constructive power of the gift of tongues to shape the future for His wonderful designs.

Paul—The Proof of the Necessity of Praying in Tongues

There is only one man in the Bible who qualifies as a candidate for us to study the effect of praying in tongues: Paul. This great apostle who, apart from Jesus, has no rival in his contribution to the Kingdom of God, spoke in tongues, in his own words, more than anyone in the entire Corinthian church. *"I thank my God I speak with tongues more than you all"* (1 Corinthians 14:18).

Because Paul spent so much time speaking in tongues, light and darkness were thoroughly parted in him by the Holy Spirit, resulting in an unmatched depth of wisdom and understanding. In fact, many people still cannot understand some of his logic. But all of his writing is based on a profound sense of reasoning—light and darkness divided.

One definition of the word *contrast* is, "the relative difference between light and dark..." (Dictionary.com). Paul's writing is self-evidently full of contrast in defining the boundaries of complex theological, spiritual, social, and moral issues. Therefore one who writes using contrast is doing so to separate the light from darkness of a subject. This contrasting style is, in fact, a main characteristic of Paul's writing. Notice the contrast: *"What shall we say then? Shall we continue in sin, that grace may abound? God forbid"* (Romans 6:1-2 KJV). He wrote of the contrast of sin vs. grace, Jew vs. Gentile, works of the flesh vs. the fruit of the Spirit, and the gifts of the Spirit vs. love.

He created, by the Holy Spirit, detailed metaphors describing the multifaceted aspects of spiritual protection and warfare such as the armor of God (Ephesians 6) and Timothy's leadership admonition of the soldier, athlete, and farmer (2 Timothy 2). This power of metaphorical images also comes from praying in tongues. Paul prayed in tongues enough to publicly state that his private use of the gift exceeded anyone in the entire Corinthian church and, as a result his light and darkness was acutely divided!

Romans 7 is really a great example of this "contrast" principle. Paul essentially writes, "I want to do right (the light), but I do not always do it (the darkness)." He also says, "I do not will to sin (the light), but I sometimes do sin (the darkness)." He finally throws himself under the bus, lamenting, "O wretched man that I am" (the darkness). He takes complete ownership of the sin within himself and humbly seeks a deliverer, "Who will deliver me from the body of this death?"

Here we also find an insightful comparison for our purposes: Paul the apostle knows he is a "wretched" man but Jesus severely threatened the church at Laodicea who considered themselves righteous but were oblivious of their "wretched" state (Revelation 3:17). The one who prays in tongues becomes aware of his own wretchedness because light and darkness are divided, but the lukewarm church needed gold tried with fire—tongues.

Next Paul goes directly from his own sin and wretchedness (Chapter 7) to the power of the Holy Spirit to mortify the deeds of the flesh (Chapter 8); even referring to the Holy Spirit speaking through us with sounds too deep for words, for example praying in tongues.

I Couldn't Help but Notice

I have already told you that after I was filled with the Holy Spirit I immediately started praying in tongues for an hour a day. This was wonderful for me because I honestly knew I was God's partner in some really important work. I had been hired by Jesus' secret service! I'm reminded of the account in Genesis when Joseph's father gave him the new exotic-looking coat—the kid never took it off! I knew inside that my Father in Heaven had given me a wonderful new mysterious code language, so I donned the coat of my new language, praying in tongues addictively.

I began timing myself to get my hour in each evening. I was taught this was expected because Jesus said to Peter when they were falling asleep in Gethsemane, *"What? Could you not watch with Me one hour? Watch and pray, lest you enter into temptation. The spirit indeed is willing, but the flesh is weak"* (Matthew 26:40-41). I also knew if one wanted to learn to play the guitar or piano, the requirement is an hour a day of practice, so why not invest at least that much time using my new God-skill?

Then, somewhere in the first year of my walk I watched a teaching on television that said, "Everyone should pray an hour a day in the Spirit, if you want average. If you want more than average, you ought to sometimes pray in the Spirit two hours a day or even three!" For me, this just added fuel to the fire.

Dr. Yonggi Cho has reported praying three hours or more daily in tongues. I invite you to enjoy this blog taken from *Fire from Heaven*, offering just a snippet of insight into what such prayer can produce:

On the verge of a sore throat, exhausted from my first day at work and the stress of yet-un-farmed-out stories, I decided to relax this evening by subscribing to TIME magazine online, and getting full access to its archives, which are rather delicious!

I pulled out many gems, among them this WONDERFUL report on Rev. David Yonggi Cho's church and the Pentecostal revival in 1973 (that's thirty-two years ago!). Rev Cho's church today is reportedly 850,000 members strong. When this article came out, it had 10,000 members!

There have been many skeptics and critics of Dr Cho's church. I personally don't have an opinion as I have not watched his TV show or read his books. All I know is that we must judge a tree by its fruit. 850,000 sounds like good fruit — but not unless Jesus is the sole and sovereign Lord of that tree!

Anyway . . . presenting:
TIME MAGAZINE

Oct. 8, 1973

Seventeen years ago, as he tells it, a young Korean named Yonggi Cho was waiting to die of tuberculosis when a girl gave him a Bible. He converted to Christianity and his tuberculosis was promptly checked, though not cured. Ordered out of his Buddhist parents' home for renouncing their faith, Cho huddled in his shabby lodgings one night, praying for a full recovery. "Suddenly the room was filled with light," he recalls. "I looked about me and saw two feet. I did not know who He was until I saw the crown of thorns piercing His temple, the blood streaming down. My lips and tongue began to speak in a strange language."

Now a robust 38, the Rev. Yonggi Cho has just finished playing host to thousands of other Christians at his 10,000-seat Full Gospel Central Church on Seoul's Yoido Island. For five days, Pentecostalists from 50 countries jammed his church for the morning sessions of the tenth triennial Pentecostal World Conference. The Seoul meeting was essentially a gathering of such "classical" Pentecostal denominations as the Assemblies of God, churches that grew out of a turn-of-the-century burst of religious enthusiasm for a direct experience of God through the Holy Spirit. Now numbering a claimed 20 million adherents worldwide, the "classicals" at the Korean conference were joined by enthusiasts from more recent Pentecostal flowerings. Many neo-Pentecostals from Presbyterian, Anglican and other mainstream churches also attended, and a sprinkling of Catholic priests in Roman collars represented the burgeoning Catholic Charismatic movement (TIME, June 18).

http://firefromheaven.blogspot.com/2005/09/dr-yonggi-cho-in-1973-time-magazine.html

---

I discovered what Pastor Cho had known for years. Praying in tongues produces good fruit. But as I started praying in tongues, I was working at the time teaching vocational printing in a New York state prison. That meant I had to work all of this new spiritual discipline around my work life, church, marriage, and raising my kids. I am a great believer that God wants to stretch us by giving us lots of plates to spin, and prioritizing those plates according to God's order is a vital lesson.

Praying in the Spirit is a discipline that is hard to justify investing your time in. There are no immediate benefits and keeping the mind fixed on God while praying in tongues for an hour or more each day takes a little practice. It is a wonderful adventure!

What Is the Measured Effect?

I knew from the moment I was filled with the Spirit that I had hold of the living God. The baptism in the Holy Spirit experience gave me a dimensional awareness I had not known before and often praying in the Spirit refilled me with the supernatural joy of the initial experience all over again. I discovered before long a church with a pastor who encouraged my thirst and helped keep me on trajectory. This pastor took me under his wing and I began a discipleship process that spurred me onward in learning the Word, conforming my life, and liberating my passion for the Spirit.

As I mentioned in Chapter Seven, Pastor Alan Babcock met with me weekly for a number of years as he would engage my questions, not taking lightly my curiosity but patiently teaching me the realm of God's Spirit. He taught me strict allegiance to God's Word and sound doctrine as the playing field of all things spiritual, a lesson I have never forsaken. He appealed to my reasoning and connected the puzzle pieces being assembled by the Holy Spirit inside.

Soon, people started remarking how I was very deep in my knowledge of God and telling me I had amazing wisdom. Although I never really felt very deep or wise, I was growing in appreciation of Jesus' depth and wisdom—and love. Honestly I was feeling most of the time how much I was not like Jesus and working to be more Christ-like in my inner life. My love for Jesus himself was in full bloom! I was captivated and connected in the deepest possible way.

A sign or mark of a life praying in the Spirit as light and darkness separate is the knowledge of one's sins and the increasing appreciation of Jesus' brilliant light. Our home became a gathering spot where friends would meet and we would talk about the Scriptures, pray, prophesy, fellowship, laugh, and generally enjoy life in the Lord for hours and hours at a time.

Up until my entrance into God's Kingdom, my life had, on some level, been awkward. As the third of seven children, I was surrounded by people for my entire life and I never lacked for friends, but honestly, I always had a sense that I didn't fit that well. My talents and gifts did not really elevate me in any identifiable way, as I was never especially "good" at anything. Then everything changed.

The day I was filled with the Holy Spirit, I realized the reason I'd been born. Everything I was inside absolutely fit with this world. I felt, at twenty-six years old, like a child prodigy and I also discovered new friends who loved the Lord just as much as I did. When we gathered together, I knew I was among my own. I was born to be a child of God.

Praying in the Spirit along with learning the Word of God during the early years enabled me to exercise and train my heart to pray. I learned to become obedient to the biblical instructions to praise, worship, give thanks, and pray in faith. I was really caught in a perfect storm of righteousness.

The house we lived in for the first five years of my walk was located on a lonely country road, and I adopted the habit of walking up and down the road in front of the house at night to pray under the stars. This work of consciously trying to engage the presence of God is an important discipline. Talking to God is not the same as talking at God. Talking to God requires practice and a willingness to push and push into a conscious sense of connection with Him.

Talking to God requires practice and a willingness to push and push into a conscious sense of connection with Him.

As You Pray for What You Want, He Will Reveal What He Wants

My formative season of prayer also had an added benefit. With an overwhelming sense of God's love for me and a realization that He could do anything, I prayed vigorously and consistently for His blessing on my life. The faith teachers taught that it is important to pray for what you want. What a wonderful premise!

Honestly, prior to meeting Jesus, I never really thought seriously or deeply about what I would like out of life if I could have anything I wanted. Just the standard American dream would do. All I really did know is that

I wanted good things for my family and now I wanted to be immersed in God's business. I remember asking Jesus for a job working for His company and began to feel like life would better if I didn't have to sleep so that I could be with Jesus all night, every night.

Funny, though I loved my pastor and held him in high regard, I didn't want to have his job in the least. I hated how ministers seemed to be treated like outsiders and his pay and benefits didn't look too appealing. In my own mind, I had a real job (I have many times since begged the Father for forgiveness for this disrespectful, unspoken attitude).

Pastor Alan and I would have our weekly meetings through the frigid winter months. He would be hunkered down behind his desk in his tiny basement office in his tiny church with a big thick sweater on and the kerosene space heater smelling up the place, trying to hold the chill back. It sort of reminded me of Bob Cratchit working for Scrooge. So in my prayer I was certainly not volunteering to be the pastor of a small country church. This joke would eventually be on me when I received my assignment of leading a tinier church in an even more remote community. (I was, by the way, elated with my good fortune!)

But praying in the Spirit and stretching my heart to look seriously into the future, daring to ask the Father for His best blessings—physically, spiritually, vocationally, relationally, and economically—produced an unanticipated benefit. In discovering who Jesus was and trying to figure how I fit into Him, I discovered, for the first time without any false faces—myself. A crystal clear self-image emerged both humble and strong as I gazed into the mirror of God's Word and prayed in the Holy Spirit. Trying to discover self by comparing oneself to other people is ultimately futile. If you're honest some people are always going to be better, some worse. Discovering self as reflected back from the face of Jesus, on the other hand, is glorious—and also painful. He is dazzling and loves passionately, but in encountering Him we are confronted by contrast with our frailty and weakness.

I realized that as I prayed in tongues and my heart probed His realm, light and darkness became more distinct from one another, separating sin from self and revealing Jesus as the true model of the ideal objective. His virtues became the treasure to be admired and coveted, and sin was no longer a secret part of my true self, but a trespasser and unwelcome virus. Whereas sin was formerly understood as the part of self that must be hidden and managed in order to keep it under wraps, now I learned that in reality, sin was an enemy invader needing to be expunged. What a joy to find out that Jesus came to deliver us from sin!

Praying in the Spirit separates the light from the darkness so the darkness becomes concentrated and clearly identifiable. The presence of God's love makes a person loathe the sin inside,

As you pray in the Spirit darkness becomes concentrated and clearly identifiable.

making repentance much more natural and desirable. The Word of God is the DNA code of the new life birthed in you, and as the Spirit moves, the code is implanted, bits becoming strands, eventually developing systems of righteous understanding and growing organically into God's Kingdom.

Also, the element of faith is integral as a person must wrestle within himself to believe this righteous self is, in fact, the true self and sin is the trespasser and the invader from hell, sent to deceive and pervert true identity. This Genesis 1 redemptive process is the master template of the organic manufacturing process of the Kingdom. Discovering one's true identity and constantly hoping for God's best for the future is integral to success.

Ask Yourself

* Will you pray in tongues to discover
   who you really are in Christ?
* Will you pray in tongues to discover what
   He really wants to do in and through you?
* Will you pray in tongues to die to
   your old self and be resurrected
   by His Spirit to new life?

Chapter Nine

MORE ZEAL THAN BRAINS

Brethren, do not be children in understanding; however, in malice be babes, but in understanding be mature.

1 Corinthians 14:20

SIGNPOST

A couple years after being filled with the Holy Spirit, I was working as a vocational printing instructor in a prison with a fellow instructor who was an atheist. Ted was the drafting instructor in the next classroom/shop over from mine and, although we were cordial, he was as passionate about his view as I was mine. He had, in fact, a plaque hanging on the wall behind his desk that said, "Reality is Change." It was his personal credo, which refers to the fluctuation between energy and matter in the physical universe. Occasionally we would have lunch together in one another's shop specifically to banter over our issues of faith.

Ted was not just someone who didn't believe, he was a God/religion hater. I, on the other hand, was really just cutting my teeth in the Lord and had way more zeal than knowledge. Ted had been chewing up and spitting out guys like me for a long time. The closest I ever came to seeing a chink in his armor was when I asked him if he really believed life had no purpose. "When you die," I asked, "is it just black nothingness?" I could see the shiver go up his spine as it hit him and he kind of weakly offered that maybe the energy collects somewhere in the universe. Both of us knew I scored a point that day because if you are going to admit something might happen after life you are saying I may well be right. And if I'm right, you're in trouble!

That was a good day. But one day Ted scored a major point against me. We were having lunch together and I shared my testimony with him. I told him Jesus saved me, miraculously set me free, filled me with His Holy Spirit, and I was given an amazing exotic prayer language from God. I told him my heart felt like brand new and it had been the most wonderful thing that ever happened to me. I told him I received the gift of tongues—an entire language system that comes from somewhere inside—and when I pray this way, I have a direct line to Heaven. I never expected Ted to ask me if I would speak in tongues out loud so he could hear it.

I made an impromptu decision. I thought, "My prayer language flows out with such grace and exotic intricacy; this might just throw old Ted for a loop and open the door for Jesus to get in." In my mind, my tongues sounded so impressive! So I opened my mouth and spoke out a good ten seconds of the most well-pronounced Holy Ghost tongues, just like I did each night in my prayer time. I certainly wouldn't say I was comfortable sharing by any stretch, but I felt on the spot and I sure wasn't ashamed, so why not? I was in new waters.

As soon as I finished, Ted smirked and, without hesitation, recited back to me with amazing fluency what sounded exactly like the same tongues I had just spoken. He told me it was nothing but gibberish and laughed in my face—we both knew he scored a point. I was bewildered. Not that it affected my faith, but because he could sound so much like my *prayer language without any infusion of the Holy Spirit behind it. Truthfully, I was as enamored with my new spiritual ability and every bit as immature in my understanding of speaking in tongues as the Christians Paul was writing to in 1 Corinthians 14. I'm still not embarrassed by my prayer language, but I have surely grown in my understanding during the thirty years since receiving it.*

Unpacking 1 Corinthians 14:1-20

The purpose of Paul's instruction in this Scripture is to bring under control the use of tongues as a public proclamation gift in church gatherings. The setting could be compared to all the members of a local church taking turns behind the microphone to deliver messages in tongues one at a time. This young church was apparently so excited about this new gift from God that many were speaking in tongues before the congregation, not really understanding the main purpose as a private devotional language.

Paul, with the true love of a father, gently corrected them in this excess. Being careful not to diminish their zeal, he lovingly brought common sense. What is especially beneficial to us is that in doing so he shared some general insight on spiritual tongues illuminating the deeper truths. Let's take it line by line:

Pursue love, and desire spiritual gifts, . . .

In 1 Corinthians 12, Paul begins a discussion on the evidences, or gifts, of the Holy Spirit manifested through believers. In Chapter 13, he makes an important contrast between the gifts and love. Love is always the most important thing, and gifts should never upstage the preeminence of love as being the Holy Spirit's objective in all things.

He opens Chapter 14 by showing that the gifts and love are not exclusive of each other, but even as love must be pursued it is perfectly expected to desire spiritual gifts—it is a normal and healthy feeling for Christians to have. This is an important point as even today many people seem unsure if and how they should approach the gifts of the Holy Spirit. Paul is very cautious not to diminish the Corinthian church's zeal for spiritual gifts.

...but especially that you may prophesy.
For he who speaks in a tongue does
not speak to men but to God,
for no one understands him;
however, in the spirit he speaks mysteries.

The end of verse one is connected with verse two because they complete a thought. This shows the context of his teaching as the use of tongues in a group setting as a proclamation gift. Holy Ghost tongues are not understood by people so there is, for the most part, little benefit to speaking in tongues publicly. Prophecy, on the other hand, is spoken in our own language and therefore people understand and are encouraged. From this verse we also learn:

1. **When speaking in tongues you are not speaking to people**. This is spiritual language spoken for spiritual purposes and scrambled to human ears but important to God.

2. **When speaking in tongues no one understands!** This is the biggest problem rationalizing the use of tongues devotionally because the mind works against faith to convince you that there is no purpose in speaking this gibberish. But we can see the gift has been this way from the beginning ... no one understands. Not even the one speaking. Much like noted previously, it is very much like the Tree of Life, fruit eaten in faith that does not fulfill any felt need.

3. **When speaking in tongues you are speaking to God.** This is a very important point because it says explicitly that speaking in tongues is prayer. "You are speaking to God." Why in the world would anyone not want to pray in tongues devotionally when Jesus died to give us a perfect, unfiltered code language that can ensure perfect prayers every time? What is surprising is how deep the human thirst for "self" causes most to become bored or disillusioned with speaking in tongues.

4. **When speaking in tongues you are speaking mysteries.** According to *Vines Expository Dictionary*,

the Greek word for "mystery" here does not speak of truth withheld but rather truth revealed. This supports our insight that speaking in tongues is loosing the activity of angels as we are pronouncing God's perfect will to the spiritual realm. It also speaks of the correlation between speaking in tongues and receiving spiritual wisdom and revelation, which is the organic by-product of tongues.

But he who prophesies speaks edification and exhortation and comfort to men.

The point of this is to teach that prophecy is for group sharing whereas speaking in tongues does not accomplish anything in a group unless followed by interpretation. There is no point speaking a language to others that no one understands.

He who speaks in a tongue edifies himself, . . .

The Greek word for "edify" is the same root as *edifice*. It means to *build something*—like a construction project or a house. Speaking in tongues as a devotional practice releases the Holy Spirit to utilize the construction material of the Word of God and build your spiritual house. Through speaking in tongues, the Holy

Speaking in tongues as a devotional practice releases the Holy Spirit to utilize the construction material of the Word of God and build your spiritual house.

Spirit illuminates and energizes the Scriptures, connecting and arranging His Kingdom within. With a teachable spirit open to God's correction, demolition is accomplished on old corrupt systems of understanding and brand new righteous perspective lights up the inner man. The Holy Spirit is free to move unobstructed by flesh or ideology and build according to God's blueprint.

This is the *coup de grace* of the Holy Ghost invasion of Earth! The Spirit-filled child of God, in a sense, builds his own house and is rewarded based on his faith effort. Praying in tongues is like peddling a bike hooked up to the generator that provides power to the construction tools. The harder and longer you peddle the faster the house goes up. You can build a great house or a small house. You can work quickly and passionately on your house, or you can live in someone else's house.

If the Lord Jesus has seen fit to restore the gift of tongues after being lost for so long, He must have some big plans. It would sure seem a shame not to be in the game.

. . . but he who prophesies edifies the church.

Again, in the context of a group setting the gift of prophecy is much more fitting because the Holy Spirit is building up others—plain and simple. Prophecy is a really cool gift given to encourage the church.

I wish you all spoke with tongues, . . .

Great line! *I wish, . . .* This is the answer to all who feel like the distribution of the gifts is some hard, fast, arbitrary predetermination of God. God will typically not invade someone's will by forcing gifts on them any more than He forces salvation on them. Salvation is exercised by faith even as the gifts are sought by faith. If the great Apostle Paul wished they all spoke in tongues, what Christian would ever think tongues are not worth seeking?

Jesus said, *"So I say to you, ask, and it will be given to you; seek, and you will find; knock, and it will be opened to you. For everyone who asks receives, and he who seeks finds, and to him who knocks it will be opened. If a son asks for bread from any father among you, will he give him a stone? Or if he asks for a fish, will he give him a serpent instead of a fish? Or if he asks for an egg, will he offer him a scorpion? If you then, being evil, know how to give good gifts to your children, how much more will your heavenly Father give the Holy Spirit to those who ask Him!"* (Luke 11:9-13, *emphasis added*).

> *...but even more that you prophesied; for he who prophesies is greater than he who speaks with tongues, unless indeed he interprets, that the church may receive edification.*

Prophecy is a group gift as tongues are a private gift **unless** someone is present to interpret. More than once my wife, Nancy, has heard someone speaking in tongues in a group meeting and distinctly heard words in English in her mind running concurrently. This is what happened on the day of Pentecost when the disciples ran out onto the street praying in tongues and all the people gathered from many nations "heard" them speaking in their own languages. The disciples were praying as the Spirit gave them utterance, but people from all over the known Earth heard them speaking their own native tongues.

But now, brethren, if I come to you speaking with tongues, what shall I profit you unless I speak to you either by revelation, by knowledge, by prophesying, or by teaching? Even things without life, whether flute or harp, when they make a sound, unless they make a distinction in the sounds, how will it be known what is piped or played? For if the trumpet makes an uncertain sound, who will prepare himself for battle? So likewise you, unless you utter by the tongue words easy to understand, how will it be known what is spoken? For you will be speaking into the air. There are, it may be, so many kinds of languages in the world, and none of them is without significance. Therefore, if I do not know the meaning of the language, I shall be a foreigner to him who speaks, and he who speaks will be a foreigner to me. Even so you, since you are zealous for spiritual gifts, let it be for the edification of the church that you seek to excel. Therefore let him who speaks in a tongue pray that he may interpret.

Paul is really being very gentle in trying to reason with the Corinthians as to why they shouldn't give orations in tongues often in their church meetings. He is lovingly comparing tongues to any foreign language or an instrument playing haphazard notes. There is just no point. No one can understand unless the sound makes sense.

Therefore to participate and help build up fellow believers it is important to seek the gifts that will allow others to understand what is being spoken. It is obvious that he does not wish to diminish their zeal for spiritual gifts. He's not trying to pop their bubble. He's trying to balance their love for tongues and set gatherings in order.

This is not surprising. When someone receives the gift of tongues there is a natural desire to share it with others. It is a crazy sensation to have words and syllables coming from your mouth but not coming from your mind. The Corinthians were not really sure what they were doing but I'll bet they were having a ball doing it. Paul was trying to bring their gatherings to a higher place of purpose.

For if I pray in a tongue, my spirit prays, . . .

Here it is! When I pray in tongues MY spirit prays. My born-again spirit is composed of the substance of eternity and therefore my spirit prays the will of the Holy Spirit who is in me. Jesus said, "...thy will be done on earth as it is in Heaven."

My spirit prays God's perfect will in His own language as the Holy Spirit gives me utterance.

God's will is perfectly expressed on Earth through tongues. My spirit prays God's perfect will in His own language as the Holy Spirit gives me utterance.

The Apostle John writes in the beginning of the Book of Revelation, *"I was in the Spirit on the Lord's Day, and I heard behind me a loud voice, as of a trumpet..."* (Revelation 1:10). This condition of being "in the Spirit" simply refers to devotionally praying in tongues. As we've been saying all along, praying in tongues requires learning to connect one's mind with God while the Spirit gives words. This creates the mental environment for visions, revelation, illumination, divine guidance, answer to prayers and so on. *If I pray in a tongue my spirit prays!*

The prophetic world beyond the eyesight is teeming with life which must be sought in the Spirit.

...but my understanding is unfruitful.

Paul is saying that he does not understand the words coming out of his mouth. They are gibberish. They make no sense. The words I speak in tongues are some foreign language from another world and my mind has no benefit because I do not understand.

What is the conclusion then? I will pray with the spirit, and I will also pray with the understanding. I will sing with the spirit, and I will also sing with the understanding. Otherwise, if you bless with the spirit, how will

he who occupies the place of the uninformed
say "Amen" at your giving of thanks, since
he does not understand what you say?

I will pray in tongues, I will pray in English, I will sing with tongues, I will sing in English. Otherwise if I'm praising God in tongues how could anyone understand me and be encouraged by my words?

For you indeed give thanks well, . . .

Praying in tongues is a great way to praise the Lord. Spiritual tongues are a great way to give thanks. It is important to engage the mind even though the mouth is speaking outside the realm of your understanding. Giving thanks, worshiping, interceding, seeking understanding, asking for blessings, praising, singing, and any other form of prayer is appropriate in the Spirit. Always pray with your understanding for what you know you want to say, and always pray in the Spirit so that God can say through you what He wants to say.

...but the other is not edified.

Paul just continues to draw contrast for the purpose of moving them away from speaking in tongues as a proclamation gift in church meetings. Other people listening do not understand what you are saying and are therefore not edified (built up).

*I thank my God I speak with
tongues more than you all;
yet in the church I would rather speak five
words with my understanding,
that I may teach others also, than
ten thousand words in a tongue.*

Earlier we had the *coup de grace.* Now this is *pièce de résistance.* We shared at the outset that the Holy Spirit, as made visible through the fluttering wings of the dove at Jesus' baptism, tongues of fire at Pentecost, and the fluttering (YLT) Spirit of God in Genesis 1:2 are fulfilled now in the gift of tongues. This makes Genesis 1 the master pattern of redemption and shows the Spirit's initial and foremost task of dividing light from darkness.

A key to Paul's great insight, resolve and depth of conviction was that he prayed in tongues—a lot! More than anyone in the entire church! Not even a contest. Alone! The Corinthians liked to showboat their tongues for others to hear thereby getting some flesh benefit out of having the most exotic sounding cool language. But Paul makes an absolute statement without even qualifying it with proof. He's like an adult speaking to little children. He's saying, "Read my lips. I THANK GOD THAT I PRAY IN TONGUES MORE THAN YOU ALL. But I do it privately."

He reemphasizes what he has been saying all along. He does not speak in tongues as a proclamation gift at a group meeting because no one understands even one word of it. It has no benefit. Even one sentence in English is more valuable than an hour's speech in tongues.

Brethren, do not be children in understanding; however, in malice be babes, but in understanding be mature.

Paul is saying this is not rocket science (although it is higher truth) so don't make it more complicated than it is. Tongues are, for the most part, a private prayer language while prophecy is for public encouragement.

Ask Yourself

* Am I praying privately in tongues for edification?
* Am I sharing prophetically what God has spoken to edify others?
* Is my attitude of praying in tongues one of humility?

*Always pray with
your understanding
for what you know
you want to say,
and always pray
in the Spirit so
that God can say
through you what
He wants to say.*

Chapter Ten

WORKING ON
A PIRATE SHIP

Go into all the world and preach the gospel to every
creature. He who believes and is baptized will be saved.

Mark 16:15-16

SIGNPOST

I worked for several years in the pre-press department
of a large commercial company specializing in high
volume, high speed, web-based products. The place
ran around the clock and employed maybe three
hundred people altogether. I had elected to work the
night shift from 7:00 p.m. to 7:00 a.m., because it
allowed more freedom to do ministry work during the

day. Besides, I always liked the night shift. In most places the atmosphere is a little more laid back and less formal than during the day shift.

Over my total of almost two decades in the printing industry, I worked in many disciplines within the printing field, both production and management, from layout and design to pre-press, press, bindery, and even shipping. This pre-press job was a desirable position in the company because, in comparison with the rest of the plant, it paid well, required skilled craftsmanship, and the staff was treated with respect. There were between five and eight of us at any given time in this department working together to prepare images for the presses.

I'll never forget talking to a coworker named Lou during a break once. I was witnessing to him about my faith in Jesus and trying my hardest to be a fisher of men. I told him my personal story of coming to faith, and when that didn't seem to affect him, I decided to turn up the heat a little. I started talking about where you go when you die and the two potential destinations for spending all of eternity. I was saying Jesus is the only name given by which men must be saved from hell and I would never want him to end up going there. Lou suddenly just looked at me and blurted, "Man, no wonder they used to throw *you guys to the lions!" I may be a little sick, but I was quite pleased with myself.*

On another occasion a guy named Tim, who was the night supervisor of the warehouse/loading dock, came through our department. He was a ZZ Top-looking-crazy man, notorious for verbally cutting people to pieces and had a very funny, albeit profane, sense of humor. When Tim came around everyone knew three things: 1) some poor soul would be his next victim; 2) most everyone else would be in stitches with laughter; and 3) the paint would be peeling off the wall from the unhindered flow of profanity.

On this particular night as Tim came walking through, I saw my coworker Lenny wave him over and whisper, pointing at me. I knew by his mischievous grin he was instigating Tim against me, telling him I was one of those "born-again" Christians and offering me up for this evening's roast. Lenny was a sour sort of guy, not a believer, and he'd enjoy throwing me to the sharks. I prepared for the worst, figuring Tim was going to humiliate and insult me. Like an innocent sailor framed by his shipmates, I was going to walk the plank as this evening's entertainment in front of a veritable pirate ship cast of co-workers.

This is where having invested time praying in the Holy Spirit will often produce surprise results. The gift of tongues is not principally for public oratory, but as you invest time praying in the Spirit, the angels go before you to prepare moments and circumstances of divine opportunity. As Tim made his way to my workstation, the sense of foreboding I felt was palpable. He bellowed with a loud voice, "So, I hear you are a 'born again' Christian" (always the sneer-like emphasis on "born again").

> **As you invest time praying in the Spirit, the angels go before you to prepare moments and circumstances of divine opportunity.**

"Yup, sure am," I said, pretending not to be feeling sick to my stomach. Then something amazing happened. Tim grabbed a stool, sat down near me and said, "Tell me about it." We began to speak as the crowd who had gathered to watch the roast slowly evaporated, disappointed at not having been entertained.

For the next forty-five minutes, we chatted as I continued to work at my light table. I felt like the angels put us in something akin to the famous "cone of silence" from **Get Smart** *(1960s vintage TV series). We were not interrupted even once as I shared the gospel, gave my testimony, and answered a bunch*

WORKING ON A PIRATE SHIP

of his questions as best I could. Tim was respectful, curious, and intelligent. He thanked me when we were done and I told him I would pray for him. Actually, I was just happy to have dodged the bullet!

Within a month or so after this encounter, we heard some bad news. Tim, who was in his mid-thirties at the most, had a terrible heart attack and was hanging at death's door. He was in critical condition for months and the report was that although Tim pulled through, his heart was badly damaged and he would never work again.

I left the printing job soon after and moved out into full time ministry, but a couple of years later returned. The young church I led was slowly but steadily growing but with a wife, five children, and one modest salary, money was just too short. The company was more than happy to hire me back and accommodate my ministry needs, which helped a lot. I spent two more years at this job before leaving again and was able to save a down payment to purchase a home.

One night soon after returning to the job, a skinny old ZZ Top-looking man walked into our department. It was Tim. He was very frail; maybe 115 pounds soaking wet and at first seemed sixty years old.

The poor guy looked terrible. He walked slow and hunched over—very sickly. Tim had been a young, robust, confident, and fast-talking guy.

He walked directly up to me and said, "I heard you were back here working and I had to talk to you. There's something you need to know." He went on, "After I had my heart attack, for months I laid in the hospital at death's door and could not even speak. During that entire time all the words you spoke to me that night kept running through my mind. I just needed for you to know that I gave my heart to Jesus and was recently baptized at my sister's church. I'm born again!"

The last I heard of Tim, now years later, is that he is still serving the Lord. This is the kind of miracle I find most satisfying in life. Jesus arranges circumstances and the angels. Like secret service agents, they sweep the area for threats so that a meeting of minds and hearts can happen with eternal results. These opportunities should be expected if one invests time praying in the Holy Spirit. Spiritual tongues empower

Like secret service agents, the angels sweep the area for threats so that a meeting of minds and hearts can happen with eternal results.

angels to go into your future, protecting you from destruction, and preparing divine intersections.

Tongues and Angels

Though I speak with the tongues of men and of angels.

1 Corinthians 13:1

Now Jacob went out from Beersheba and went toward Haran. So he came to a certain place and stayed there all night, because the sun had set. And he took one of the stones of that place and put it at his head, and he lay down in that place to sleep. Then he dreamed, and behold, a ladder was set up on the earth, and its top reached to heaven; and there the angels of God were ascending and descending on it. And behold, the Lord stood above it and said: "I am the Lord God of Abraham your father and the God of Isaac; the land on which you lie I will give to you and your descendants. Also your descendants shall be as the dust of the earth; you shall spread abroad to the west and the east, to the north and the south; and in you and in your seed all the families of the earth shall be blessed. Behold, I am with you and will keep you wherever you go, and will bring you back to this land; for I will not leave you until I have done what I have spoken to you." Then Jacob awoke from his sleep and said, "Surely the Lord is in this place, and I did not know it." And he was afraid and said, "How awesome is this place! This is none other than the house of God, and this is the gate of heaven!" Then Jacob rose early in the morning, and took the stone that he had put at his head, set it up as a pillar, and poured oil on top of it.

Genesis 28:10-18

And He said to him, "Most assuredly, I say to you, hereafter you shall see heaven open, and the angels of God ascending and descending upon the Son of Man."

John 1:51

The audacious account of "Blind Bartimaeus" is told in Mark 10. The story tells of a blind man crying out to Jesus for help as the Master's entourage passes by on the road coming from Jericho. Bartimaeus puts up such a raucous display that his friends shush him, which he completely ignores, and continues to bellow at the top of his lungs, "Jesus, son of David, have mercy on me!" His unrelenting efforts impress Jesus, stopping Him in His tracks, and Bartimaeus receives the miracle of his sight restored.

We are now like Blind Bartimaeus. We are blind to Jesus' realm and entourage passing by. The Scripture testifies of the presence of angels, demons, the Holy Spirit, Jesus, and even Satan inhabiting the heavenly airspace all around us but we are physically blind to their presence. They are matters of faith. Like Bartimaeus, we now have to call out to Jesus in our blindness depending on our faith through the testimony of Scripture and others.

Among the central players in the Father's master plan to free His children from Satan's death grip are the angels of God. Angels are cited as important messengers, warriors, and agents of God's Kingdom throughout the Scriptures. Like other spiritual entities, they are invisible (except on special occasions) to our physical eyes. These spiritual secret agents are behind the scenes throughout the Old and New Testaments doing God's bidding in a lot of different ways.

For our consideration the Gospel of John recounts the following:

> *Jesus saw Nathanael coming toward Him, and said of him, "Behold, an Israelite indeed, in whom is no deceit!" Nathaniel said to Him, "How do You know me?" Jesus answered and said to him, "Before Philip called you, when you were under the fig tree, I saw you." Nathanael answered and said to Him, "Rabbi, You are the Son of God! You are the King of Israel!" Jesus answered and said to him, "Because I said to you, 'I saw you under the fig tree,' do you believe? You will see greater things than these." And He said to him, "Most assuredly, I say to you, hereafter you shall see heaven open, and the angels of God ascending and descending upon the Son of Man."*

> John 1:47-51

First of all, Jesus implicitly says that the prophetic information He shared with Nathaniel was given to Him by angels. These are not two statements disconnected from each other, but the reference to the angels is built on Nathaniel's knee-jerk response to Jesus' divine insight. Jesus is saying, "The angelic workers are going to deliver to me unlimited heavenly power through supernatural knowledge, signs, wonders, and miracles." That is what the angels do. They deliver God's messages and His power. They arrange divine encounters.

Angels deliver God's messages and His power. They arrange divine encounters.

Secondly, the statement Jesus makes about the angels of God ascending and descending is a direct reference to Jacob's ladder, a very important prophetic precedent. Jacob's ladder is, in fact, a prophecy of Jesus as God's ultimate plan to invade planet Earth reclaiming this exiled rock for His own glory. Also, as the Tower of Babel represents unified human genius and effort climbing a tower of knowledge to access higher power, Jacob's dream represents Jesus—God's plan to reach down to humans through the frailty of His Son's broken body and spilled blood. As cited earlier in this book, both operations include the introduction of new tongues. Whereas Babel's tongues were confused to create disunity, Pentecost's tongues, as displayed upon the crowd gathered outside, were destined to produce the unity of the faith.

Babel's tongues were confused to create disunity, Pentecost's tongues were destined to produce the unity of the faith.

When Jacob falls asleep with his head on the rock, his dream depicts the heavens open and the angels of God ascending and descending up and down a ladder. At the same time God is speaking from the top announcing His plans for the future. (It is of paramount importance that we stay within the safety of God's written Word. We never advocate the Spirit without the Word, they are always in unity.) Jacob wakes up and announces this place as the gate of Heaven. He then takes the rock he rested on and sets it up as a memorial. Next he pours oil on the rock; this is the first occasion of anointing in the Bible.

Note the wording, "poured oil on top of it." The prophetic picture Jacob created was a flowing stream of oil from the vessel to the rock, capturing the living stream of angels moving up and down from Heaven. Angels go up carrying prayers and come down to carry out God's Word. Whereas Jesus was the rock on which the flow of angels poured without measure, the Spirit now coordinates the flow to and from Heaven through the body of Christ. The gift of tongues is the activation of that flow.

The prophetic comparison is compelling. God speaking from Heaven now through our mouths as the Spirit gives utterance. Paul said we're speaking with the tongues of angels. This shows that, as our bodies are the temples of the Holy Spirit, our mouths are the gates of Heaven and therefore our spiritual tongues are given that the angels can freely flow coordinated on Earth in their own language doing God's business. Tongues empower angels.

Speaking in tongues is putting God in control. Speaking in tongues is laying down your own life, your will, and deferring to the Spirit. Speaking in tongues empowers the angels of God. We must not forget the Genesis 1:2 precedent where the Spirit of God is moving (hovering, fluttering). The Spirit MUST move on Earth. The Scriptures are full of prophecies of moving, flowing, fluttering, and pouring pictures looking forward to Holy Spirit tongues.

Joshua confronts the Commander of the Army of God and asks, "Are you for us or for our enemies?" "NO" comes the answer. God is neither for us nor for our enemies, but we are invited to join His side. Joshua then takes instruction to march around the city for six days and on the seventh to blow trumpets and have the whole army yell a great shout. The human army shouts as the angel army of the Lord knocks over the walls so God's plan can move forward. The trumpet blast and inarticulate shout prophesies of tongues empowering angels.

A cherub (angel) with a flaming sword is put on guard to keep man away from the Tree Of Life after the fall. This is remedied by God in the upper room on the day of Pentecost: The angel's wings and flaming sword "turning every which way" create rushing wind and tongues of fire as we now pass through the gate and have access to the Tree of Life, Jesus!

Now, as we eat of the Tree of Life (John 6), rivers of living water will flow out of our innermost being—tongues! Jesus is the Tree of Life. The gift of tongues uses our bodies as channels of God's power as He directs His holy angels to do His bidding.

Ask Yourself

* Are the angels of God at work in your situations and circumstances doing God's bidding?
* Are you sensitive to and aware of the spiritual realm all around you?
* Are you a channel of God's living waters allowing all of Heaven to involve you in God's bidding?

Chapter Eleven

FINAL WORD

I pray this book has ignited or reignited or relit a desire in you to pray in the tongues as a lifelong devotional practice. If you do not have the gift of tongues, I encourage you to seek it. Praying in tongues is vital to your spiritual health and growth. It is the easiest thing you can do with the greatest results. Praying in tongues creates the "wow factor" of Christian life! It opens up a portal to Heaven so that God can do His business through your body. When you pray in tongues, you become an angel airport. Praying in tongues separates inner light from darkness resulting in wisdom, revelation, humility, and power. It is the active presence of God moving within our bodies and we are changed from glory to glory even as creation was made from day to day. Praying in tongues moves angels, paves one's future, opens the Word of God, and creates destiny.

Regular people are spiritually hungry today. Churches seem to be working harder than ever, but the experienced connection with the living God seems to be upstaged by everything but Him ... "Lights, cameras, action!" They call us winners, but most are in bondage as sinners. Only one power sent by Jesus baffles the senses, makes wise men fools, and brings God's dimension to bear—anytime, anywhere, by anyone. Holy Spirit tongues!

I deeply appreciate you taking the time to consider this material. I pray you take it to heart. I recommend you start immediately praying in tongues one hour each day. It is best if you block out a regular daily time when it will cause the least disruption in your life and for family members. If you have to stay up an hour later, get up an hour earlier, use your lunch break, or sacrifice an hour after dinner, do it. The devil will fight you for it at first, but when you clear the space in the Spirit, it will become your favorite hour of the day. When you've been praying in tongues for an hour each day, after a month or two, if something disrupts your schedule, like Adam hearing God calling in the Garden, you'll hear God calling to your meeting time. You will cultivate a daily meeting you will never want to lose.

Praying in tongues will revolutionize your life.

Praying in tongues will revolutionize your life. It does not replace any other vital

Christian practice, but adds the dimension missing from most lives: true living connection with God with all of the expected evidence and deep satisfaction that comes when you are in perfect peace with God. Please, when praying in tongues devotionally, do not neglect to engage your mind. Stretch, believe, hope, and stay ever alert as the Spirit of God moves across the face of the waters. Pray on!

APPENDIX

POINTS OF ILLUMINATION

1. Jesus said, *"The wind blows where it wishes, and you hear the sound of it, but cannot tell where it comes from and where it goes. So is everyone who is born of the Spirit."* —John 3:8

   This is a great prophecy of tongues. Jesus said, like the wind, the "sound" of the Holy Spirit can be heard! Speaking in tongues signifies the audible presence of the Holy Spirit but no one knows its source (where it comes from) or its purpose (where it is going) except by faith. Jesus said this would be a mark of everybody born of the Kingdom.

2. *But you, when you pray, go into your room, and when you have shut your door, pray to your Father who is in the secret place; and your Father who sees in secret will reward you openly.* —Matthew 6:6

   Speaking in tongues is mainly for private devotional prayer. You do not understand what you are saying but it does require your heart to be connected. Jesus said "the Kingdom of God is within you" so speaking in tongues requires you to look to God's realm from within and use your own breath as an agent of the wind of the Spirit. As you spend time praying in the Spirit, the Spirit separates light from darkness, illuminates Scriptures, answers prayer, gives prophetic insight, increases faith, and makes divine connections of understanding.

It is far easier to have visions when your eyes and other senses are not distracted by your surroundings. Your inner room represents a place where your attention is not diverted by your senses and you can look within for God.

Open reward is the sure mark when you diligently exercise your faith by praying in tongues as a devotional practice. My life has been consistently blessed beyond any measure of investment I've made; most times, in spite of me. Invest in the Spirit—receive from the Spirit.

3. *So they came to Jerusalem. Then Jesus went into the temple and began to drive out those who bought and sold in the temple, and overturned the tables of the money changers and the seats of those who sold doves. And He would not allow anyone to carry wares through the temple. Then He taught, saying to them, "Is it not written, 'My house shall be called a house of prayer for all nations'? But you have made it a 'den of thieves.'"* —Mark 11:15-17

The children of God are now the temple of the Holy Spirit and the international prayer language of the New Covenant temple of God is spiritual tongues. Our inner money changers will be driven from inside by the whip of the Lord; the Spirit confronting our inner darkness. The Lord chastises those He loves.

By the way, it is amazing how similar Jesus' harshness to the money changers is to His words of warning against the rich church at Laodicea. Both involved money.

4. *And this is the condemnation, that the light has come into the world, and men loved darkness rather than light, because their deeds were evil. For everyone practicing evil hates the light and does not come to the light, lest his deeds should be exposed. But he who does the truth comes to the light, that his deeds may be clearly seen, that they have been done in God."* —John 3:19-21

You can't pray in tongues very much until you develop love for the Truth. When you pray in tongues, inner secret motives are revealed and deeply held affections for the world will revolt against the Spirit and drive you away from the practice of praying in tongues devotionally. Only your inner desire for righteousness above all things will keep you praying in tongues regularly as part of your devotion. The Spirit energizing God's Word inside exposes falsehood and confirms righteousness, separating light from darkness. The Holy Spirit cleanses and a great desire to do righteousness will take over your heart as sin practices are made issue of and eliminated.

5. *So He himself often withdrew into the wilderness and prayed.* —Luke 5:16

Solitude is an important aspect in praying in tongues. It is an important skill to develop as it requires a particular kind of communicating ... a mostly inward mental focus based on faith in the unseen realm. As you pray in tongues, your mind is focused and kept in safe boundaries through the Word of God.

Recognizing the benefit of solitude, the Yoido Full Gospel Church in Korea owns a prayer mountain with 200 private prayer chambers where people can come to spend extended time in prayer. The founder, Dr. David Cho, has built perhaps the largest church in the world with a strong emphasis on praying in tongues.

6. *"...to know the love of Christ which passes knowledge; that you may be filled with all the fullness of God."* —Ephesians 3:19

How can someone know something that surpasses knowledge? Well, it actually means to experience

APPENDIX

something you can't really understand. The Book of Romans says this love flows into our hearts by the Holy Spirit, "because the love of God has been poured out in our hearts by the Holy Spirit who was given to us" (Romans 5:5). The way the Holy Spirit flows through our bodies is by speaking in tongues.

This is the power of illumination. Praying in the Spirit (tongues), living in Christ, and abiding in the Word of God strengthens your inner man with enlightenment of things beyond knowledge. Speaking in tongues is trusting beyond your knowledge because you cannot understand what the Spirit is saying. The forbidden tree satisfied the hunger for knowledge. The Tree of Life requires sustained faith in the unseen realm.

7. *"To what shall we liken the kingdom of God? Or with what parable shall we picture it? It is like a mustard seed which, when it is sown on the ground, is smaller than all the seeds on earth; but when it is sown, it grows up and becomes greater than all herbs, and shoots out large branches, so that the birds of the air may nest under its shade."* —Mark 4:30-32

Praying in tongues is farm work—like raising crops. It does not change you overnight. It is not a lucky rabbit's foot you can pull out for immediate dramatic effect, then put away again. Praying in tongues is for life that flows from the Spirit of God in time. As the mustard seeds of God's Word are sown and the Spirit works within you through tongues, the crusty husks of the seed are eroded by the acidic soil of the soul. This reaction occurs as the light of Jesus collides with sin that dwells within. In time the husks break down and roots begin to go down and a precious shoot breaks the surface. Eventually the plant of righteousness grows to dominate the soul.

8. *For in six days the LORD made the heavens and the earth, the sea, and all that is in them, and rested the seventh day.* —Exodus 20:11

   But we all, with unveiled face, beholding as in a mirror the glory of the Lord, are being transformed into the same image from glory to glory, just as by the Spirit of the Lord. —2 Corinthians 3:18

In Genesis 1, the moving Spirit of God creates the heavens and Earth, bringing God's Word into the material world day by day, or in other words, from glory (it is good) to glory (it is good). This shows an important aspect of praying in tongues—time. The effect of praying in tongues takes time and effort. The effort is faith effort. The effort is righteousness effort. The effort is inner honesty effort as we behold God's perfect image in light of our own frailty and continue to reach for Him. In time, no different from Genesis 1, we will be brought to new glories.

Also as God created specific aspects of creation on each day based on His own will, we must know that He will do the same with us. God will not always fix you in the area you feel is most important today. He may need to do something else altogether and not want to focus on you where you would like Him to. Take a lesson from Jacob and wrestle with God for what you want—and enjoy what He is doing in the season.

9. *Likewise the Spirit also helps in our weaknesses. For we do not know what we should pray for as we ought, but the Spirit himself makes intercession for us with groanings which cannot be uttered.* —Romans 8:26

Spiritual effort. Paul, in discussing the Holy Spirit, says there is a groaning aspect to spiritual language and he associated it with the birth pangs of creation longing for the manifestation of the sons of God. Jesus prayed with great effort in Gethsemane, so much so that He was sweating blood. Elijah prayed so hard it stopped raining. Then he prayed so hard that it started again. Praying in tongues takes faith effort.

I blasted out like a shot of the cannon when I was filled with the Holy Spirit in November 1982. I prayed in the Spirit with great effort with my will and stretched my mind to engage this new Kingdom I'd discovered. As I prayed late one evening pushing and pushing into the Spirit, suddenly the inner movie screen of my mind's eye began rolling video tape that I was not producing. It took off on its own. I saw a pen begin to write on a paper. In what looked like golden luminescent ink, very slowly and decisively the name Charles F. Engelhardt was written out.

Charles F. Engelhardt is my oldest brother's name as distinct from Charles J. Engelhardt, my dad. I thanked the Lord for this cool vision and prayed for this miracle as my brother was not yet saved. Within weeks there was a Christian breakfast event on a Saturday morning at a local restaurant. My brother got wonderfully saved and filled with the Spirit. Today, he is a pastor.

I have had many experiences like this over the years, and they are the direct effect of speaking in tongues and inwardly groping for God. The more effort put into praying in the Spirit, the more supernatural results are experienced. This is faith work—effort. It is not based on impressive talents, religious qualities, or knowledge. It is pure faith stretching to believe and engage the unseen realm. A small child exerts this power when he wants his bottle. The only difference is this is rewarded by God.

10. *So then, because you are lukewarm, and neither cold nor hot, I will vomit you out of My mouth.*
—Revelation 3:16

Lukewarm Laodicea (Revelation 3) is counseled first of all to buy gold tried with fire. The fire is the fire of the Holy Spirit that came down on Pentecost (Acts 2) and our purified human soul is the gold. Praying in tongues is the fire of God heating up our inner man causing the impurities to rise to the top so we can skim them off—leaving purified gold.

11. *Then He came to the disciples and found them asleep, and said to Peter, "What! Could you not watch with Me one hour? Watch and pray, lest you enter into temptation. The spirit indeed is willing, but the flesh is weak."* —Matthew 26:40-41

The spirit is willing. Your born-again spirit is always in agreement with the Holy Spirit. Therefore, the Holy Spirit wills to pray and your spirit agrees. *Young's Literal Translation* renders this: "The spirit indeed is forward, but the flesh weak." The spirit is forward. The deepest you *wants* to pray ahead into your future, but the weakness of the flesh prevents it. Praying in the Spirit takes faith. It could be that the lack you experience now is the result of prayerlessness in the past.

12. *And they heard the sound of the LORD God walking in the garden in the cool of the day, and Adam and his wife hid themselves from the presence of the LORD God among the trees of the garden. Then the LORD God called to Adam and said to him, "Where are you?"* —Genesis 3:8-9

Jesus is the Tree of Life. The way we eat the tree is by exercising our faith in Him. He sent the gift of tongues and therefore praying in tongues is an exercise of faith in Jesus speaking the language of the Spirit. When you speak in tongues each day, clearing a daily plot of time in your life to be together, if circumstances arise making you miss your appointment with God you will distinctly hear His voice calling you. It is an uncanny feeling, but also very comforting. It leaves you a sense of God's mutual enjoyment of your time together.

13. *So when the woman saw that the tree was good for food, that it was pleasant to the eyes, and a tree desirable to make one wise, she took of its fruit and ate.* —Genesis 3:6

The New Testament confirms the human values attractive at the forbidden tree are the same values opposed to God's Kingdom today:

For all that is in the world—the lust of the flesh, the lust of the eyes, and the pride of life—is not of the Father but is of the world. —1 John 2:16

Praying in the Spirit opposes these values. Praying in tongues draws on faith, hope, and love. Praying in tongues is done in secret. When God's reward does show up in your life, be sure that people will explain it away. You will not get anyone's spiritual medal for speaking in tongues. As a matter of fact, tongues cause the opposite reaction from people. At best they will think you are a little strange, and at worst they will consider you a dangerous religious lunatic. The carnal mind revolts against tongues.

Praying in tongues does not make you smart, is not good for your health, and does not change your appearance. It is sown privately for rewards that come publicly. It requires a commitment to be alone with God. It is the most wonderful adventure you'll ever take.

14. *And because you are sons, God has sent forth the Spirit of His Son into your hearts, crying out, "Abba, Father!"* —Galatians 4:6

For you did not receive the spirit of bondage again to fear, but you received the Spirit of adoption by whom we cry out, "Abba, Father." —Romans 8:15

Vine's Expository Dictionary of Old and New Testament Words describes the usage of the word *Abba*: "It is the word framed by the lips of infants, and betokens unreasoning trust; 'father' expresses an intelligent apprehension of the relationship. The two together express the love and intelligent confidence of the child."

Paul wrote, *"I will pray with the spirit, and I will also pray with the understanding. I will sing with the spirit, and I will also sing with the understanding"*

(1 Corinthians 14:15). Speaking in tongues is an expression of childlike faith and praying with the understanding (intelligence) is conscious conversation with God in your own language.

I have a good friend who was stricken with encephalitis, an acute infection in the brain, while on a mission to Belarus in the early 1990s. By a miracle of God, he made it home on his own after spending over a week alone in a Minsk hotel room with this infection raging and no medical attention. By the time he was back home and admitted to the hospital, his short term memory was so damaged he couldn't remember any names of people, places, or things. He couldn't carry on even a simple two-way conversation except to answer *yes* and *no*.

But he could still pray in tongues! And pray he did! I will never forget the articulate words of the Spirit's language rolling from his lips in that bed even though he could hardly utter a word in English. We have been given the Spirit whereby we cry out, "Abba, Father," so when your intelligence fails you and words won't come to describe your pain, leave it to the Holy Ghost and pray in tongues. My friend's memory vastly improved with much prayer over time. The upshot of this terrible season is that he has continued to invest much time in the language of the Holy Spirit and has become an amazing world-class intercessor.

15. *"the Spirit of God moved..."* —Genesis 1:2 KJV

   "God said..." —Genesis 1:3

   Genesis 1 is the Word of God. Jesus personally put on the coat of Genesis 1 when He moved across the waters as darkness covered the deep. There is no coincidence here. This first chapter of Scripture is the master pattern of redemption. It tells how God invades, divides, and produces new multi-layered systems of life and goodness.

   There are only two components to creation: the moving Spirit and the spoken words of God. These two are in perfect agreement. The Spirit of God moves as we pray in tongues and God speaks as we abide in His Word (Jesus).

16. *But its swamps and marshes will not be healed; they will be given over to salt.*   —Ezekiel 47:11

   Ezekiel 47 tells a vision of a river flowing from beneath the Temple of God, flowing along a watercourse growing deeper and giving life to all along its path and in its waters. Notice *flowing* (verse 1). This represents the Holy Spirit in motion: *tongues.* The only places along the watercourse not healed are where the water is not flowing in swamps and marshes. These places are given over to salt. We pray in tongues so that the water can flow through our lives. Death from too much salt comes from the Scripture alone and not enough of the flowing Holy Spirit. That is why church movements tend to solidify. It is like Lot's wife who stopped moving forward to look back and turned into a pillar of salt. Same principle.

The Spirit must move!

17. *Then she lulled him to sleep on her knees, and called for a man and had him shave off the seven locks of his head. Then she began to torment him, and his strength left him. And she said, "The Philistines are upon you, Samson!" So he awoke from his sleep, and said, "I will go out as before, at other times, and shake myself free!" But he did not know that the LORD had departed from him.* —Judges 16:19-20

From the time he was born Samson never had a haircut. His supernatural strength was dependent on this and in a moment of weakness, he finally confessed to Delilah, "If I am shaven, then my strength will leave me, and I shall become weak, and be like any other man" (Judges 16:17).

The hair of Christianity is the Bible because it is an unbroken strand of genealogies from the apostles back to "the beginning" (Genesis 1) of creation. Cut off Genesis 1—the root of all Scripture—and you've cut the secret power source of Christianity. The intellectual elite of Christianity seems to have rolled over on this vital foundation of Scripture leaving them (prophetically) blind, bound by political correctness (as the Philistines) and weak, like any other man.

Without full confidence in our Scripture there is no supernatural strength. Without Genesis 1, we do not see the vital need for the moving (*fluttering*) Spirit of God and feel like the gift of tongues is optional. Without Genesis 1, we have a God bound by human understanding.

18. *So Gideon and the hundred men who were with him came to the outpost of the camp at the beginning of the middle watch, just as they had posted the watch; and they blew the trumpets and broke the pitchers that were in their hands. Then the three companies blew the trumpets and broke the pitchers—they held the torches in their left hands and the trumpets in their right hands for blowing—and they cried, "The sword of the* LORD *and of Gideon!" And every man stood in his place all around the camp; and the whole army ran and cried out and fled.* —Judges 7:19-21

Gideon's great victory over the Midianites consisted of 300 men, torches, clay pots, and trumpets. The cracked pots are the human vessels broken in repentance. The fire is the fire of the Holy Spirit (Pentecost). The trumpets are a prophetic foreshadow of Holy Ghost tongues, an inarticulate sound that confuses and terrifies the enemy. Speaking in tongues causes bedlam in the enemy camp because angels are rallied to battle in their own language (1 Corinthians 13:1) and demons are confused.

19. *Then one of the seraphim flew to me, having in his hand a live coal which he had taken with the tongs from the altar. And he touched my mouth with it, and said: "Behold, this has touched your lips; Your iniquity is taken away, And your sin purged."* —Isaiah 6:6-7

Isaiah 6 tells of a mighty vision of the throne room of God and Isaiah's experience there. The incredible glory, majesty, and holiness of God causes Isaiah to completely fall apart. But interesting for our purpose is his immediate recognition of his (and everyone he knows) dirty mouth (verse 5). Bedrock truth: human languages are not sufficient to worship God!

Next, a seraphim with three sets of wings retrieves a coal from the altar and touches Isaiah's lips. Two wings cover the angel's feet and two wings cover the angel's face leaving two wings to fly. The face covering wings and feet covering wings represent the invisibility of the Holy Spirit and the flying wings create a rushing mighty wind as heard on the day of Pentecost. The coal foretells of the tongues of fire resting on the disciples

(Acts 2) and his cleansed lips represent the gift of tongues. He received a pure language.

The bottom line is humans need a language holy enough to worship God. Isaiah's prophecy looks ahead in time when God would cleanse lips by giving a new language, not flowing from the unclean human heart but directly from the heart of God—tongues.

20. *And he touched my mouth with it, and said: "Behold, this has touched your lips; your iniquity is taken away, and your sin purged." Also I heard the voice of the Lord, saying: "Whom shall I send, and who will go for Us?" Then I said, "Here am I! Send me." And He said, "Go, and tell this people: 'Keep on hearing, but do not understand; Keep on seeing, but do not perceive.' Make the heart of this people dull, and their ears heavy, And shut their eyes; lest they see with their eyes, and hear with their ears, and understand with their heart, and return and be healed."*
   —Isaiah 6:7-10

In the preceding point we discussed the prophetic foreshadowing of the gift of tongues from the first section of Isaiah 6. This point picks up when Isaiah has had his lips cleansed and describes what comes next. We can follow this as also foretelling what will happen when people do receive spiritual tongues. This Scripture offers great insight into why people are not more enthusiastic about praying in the Spirit.

The message speaks right to the heart of the issue:

Keep on hearing, but do not understand: We hear speaking in tongues with our ears but because we do not understand the words, our hearts are resistant to believe. The heart engaged with the Spirit must be alive with enthusiastic trust that God is pouring out from within—that rivers of living water are flowing from our innermost beings. Without this faith the inner lazy, suspicious, and logical man takes over and unbelief erodes enthusiasm resulting in a dull heart. Spiritual tongues are the most important and significant spiritual practice available to humans. It is God doing His own business on Earth.

Keep on seeing, but do not perceive: We see in the Bible new tongues announced by Jesus, received by the apostles and encouraged by Paul, but do not open our eyes and understand that God has given this gift so that He might have partners to share His Kingdom with—both here on Earth and throughout eternity. God works through partners! Sow to the Spirit, reap from the Spirit. Exercising the Spirit is how you become a son of God.

"Make the heart of this people dull, and their ears heavy, and shut their eyes; lest they see

with their eyes, and hear with their ears, and understand with their heart, and return and be healed." The ears and eyes of faith must be opened in order to understand what God is doing through the gift of tongues. Dulled enthusiasm for praying in tongues assaults everyone who possesses this great ability. We must push through a spirit of slumber that works to impede these rivers of living water.

21. *So the people shouted when the priests blew the trumpets. And it happened when the people heard the sound of the trumpet, and the people shouted with a great shout, that the wall fell down flat. Then the people went up into the city, every man straight before him, and they took the city.* —Joshua 6:20

They marched around the walls of Jericho in silence for six days. On the seventh day, the priests blew trumpets, the army of Israel shouted, and the monstrous city walls fall down. Prophetically the silence is the time until this season when the Church gets a revelation of the power of spiritual tongues. The trumpets and shouting are prophetic of tongues: inarticulate sound empowering angels. The walls did not fall from human power. Joshua's encounter with the commander of the army of the Lord indicates that it was a joint mission of the people doing the trumpet blowing and shouting, and angels who did the work. Tongues and the activity of angels are tied closely together.

22. *For in six days the Lord made the heavens and the earth, the sea, and all that is in them.* — Exodus 20:11

The Fabric of Time: A component of Genesis 1 that speaks to our framework for understanding the gift of tongues is time. Some teach that time is of no consequence in the things of the Spirit (and this is true on a level) but Genesis 1 shows that time—day by day, evening by evening, and morning by morning, is absolutely a vital aspect of the pre-planned construct of God's creative process. God's spoken Word going forth, the dynamic Spirit moving, water and dry land, working from morning to evening, for six distinct segments of time.

Jesus told us of the importance of time when He spoke of the Kingdom of God as a mustard seed. It starts as a tiny organic capsule and grows—over time, intentionally—into a wonderful predetermined new creation. Like a bare tomato seed grows into the picture on the outside of the seed packet, so God's seed grows into the image of Christ. Creation is rendered from day to day; the Holy Spirit in motion, dividing light and darkness, water from dry land, and forming the spoken Word of God in matter, time, and space. The Holy Spirit hovers between time and timeless eternity turning eternal words into cosmic reality. He is the portal. As in Genesis, we now in the New Covenant are changed from glory to glory, even as by the Spirit of God (2 Corinthians 3:18). Time is a major part of the operation.

The reason time must be considered is so that we understand the importance of praying in tongues consistently for long seasons before a benefit is realized. Also, the written Word of God must be learned and digested because this is the genetic code and raw material of revelation. For the person praying in tongues to expect an immediate result is like asking for an immediate result from a planted seed. Not going to happen. It takes time.

It is interesting to note that at the end of each creative day in Genesis, God pronounces, "It is good." It is the same as achieving the glory to glory status in the New Testament. When God finishes a season in our life, He pronounces, "It is good," completing one glory, imparting a blessing, and moving us into the next reconstruction project. A main point we learn is not to resent the time it takes to continue to pray in the Spirit before the day's full glory manifests.

Now you know the Scriptural basis for praying in tongues devotionally. It is present at the beginning of Genesis and runs unbroken throughout the Bible. You have experienced a portion of my own personal testimony, and can clearly see the power you have access to if you will only discipline your flesh and exercise this amazing gift of God's Spirit to communicate with Heaven. I charge you to change how you think about praying in tongues. I urge you to activate this practice and create a new and fruitful discipline in your Christian life. Try it and see. Commit to a prolonged season of praying in tongues alone, privately, and see what God will ignite in your life and the lives of those around you. No longer hidden for you, tongues are now in plain view.

ABOUT THE AUTHOR

Robert A. Engelhardt

Noted for his biblical insight and ability to make complex truth understandable, Robert Engelhardt has had a prolific career for more than twenty-five years as a writer, speaker, radio personality, and church-building pastor. He is founding leader of FaithConnect, an association of Christian leaders, and senior pastor of Catskill Mountain Christian Center, a church and human service organization in Margaretville, NY.

Engelhardt has been on radio for two decades hosting a weekly Sunday morning broadcast and for several years as a personality on daily call-in radio. He has interviewed newsmakers, Christian leaders, and many book authors, pioneering evangelistic radio programming on secular commercial stations in his region.

Engelhardt is a frequent speaker at men's conferences and churches, and has been a guest on *The 700 Club* with Pat Robertson. He has written for *Ministries Today* magazine and revised and edited two *Pure Gold Classic* books for national publication. Mission work has taken him to many nations in the world with a twenty-year ongoing concentration on Kenya.

Having planted churches and developing leaders, Bob has seen the need for leaders to be in relationship. To that end, FaithConnect network was founded in 2009 under Engelhardt's apostolic leadership. FaithConnect is an organization for Christian leaders who share the vision of being culturally relevant, biblically sound, and genuinely connected.

As a husband, father, and leader, Bob has known good times, bad times, and miracles alike. His depth of experience allows others to engage the supernatural in completely natural, non-mystical ways.

Married since 1977, Bob and his wife, Nancy, have four sons, a daughter, and four grandchildren. He is a member of the International Coalition of Apostles and Open Bible Faith Fellowship of Canada. He is a board member of CitiHope International, and Alight Care Center.

Also by Robert Engelhardt

White Like Snow
Reflections on Living Through Your Seasons

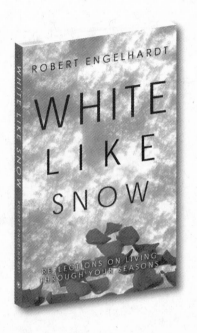

Life is filled with seasons. Learning how to recognize the season you are in and prepare for the season that is coming will help you develop a successful rhythm for your life. This collection of articles by Robert Engelhardt addresses many of life's seasons with gentle wisdom, experience, and understanding. You are right where you need to be in order to fulfill your unique destiny. Nothing in your past dictates what must happen in your future.

When you allow God to prepare you for each season of growth, though your sins be as scarlet, He will wash you white as snow.

Whatever life sends your way, you will be able to walk through it all with grace and victory.

For more information, please visit:

www.cmcconline.org

www.faithconnect.org